CRISIS IN THE WEST

By the same author

THE RISE OF ANGLO-AMERICAN FRIENDSHIP (1938; 1966)

PEACE BY POWER (1942)

REPRIEVE FROM WAR (1950)

THE AMERICAN ANARCHY (1953)

AMERICA IN BRITAIN'S PLACE (1961)

THE ALLIANCE OF NECESSITY (1966; 1967)

CRISIS IN THE WEST

American Leadership and the Global Balance

LIONEL GELBER

[redacted]

M

First published 1975 by
THE MACMILLAN PRESS LTD
London and Basingstoke
Associated companies in New York
Dublin Melbourne Johannesburg and Madras

SBN 333 17789 4

Typeset by
COLD COMPOSITION LTD
Southborough, Tunbridge Wells

Printed in Great Britain by
REDWOOD BURN LIMITED
Trowbridge and Esher

Contents

Acknowledgements

The writer wishes to express his thanks to editors who have been good enough to permit the republication of articles on which most, but not all, of this book has been based. Their journals are as follows:

Contemporary Review, London, with which the *Fortnightly,* London, was incorporated (Chapter 1); the *Virginia Quarterly Review,* a National Journal of Literature and Discussion, Charlottesville, Virginia (Chapter 2); the *New Leader,* New York (Chapter 3); *Christianity and Crisis,* New York (Chapters 4 and 5); *Orbis,* a Journal of World Affairs, published by The Foreign Policy Research Institute, University of Pennsylvania, Philadelphia (Chapters 6 and 9); the *Spectator,* London (Chapters 7, 8, 13 and 15); the *Antioch Review,* an Independent Quarterly Journal, copyright © 1953 by The Antioch Review Inc., Yellow Springs, Ohio (Chapter 10); *Foreign Affairs,* copyrighted by Council on Foreign Relations, Inc., New York (Chapter 11); the *Yale Review,* a National Quarterly, copyright The Yale University Press, New Haven, Conn. (Chapter 12); *Pacific Community,* An Asian Quarterly Review, Jiji Press, Tokyo (Chapter 14).

One further debt must be recorded. It is to Mr Hugh Corbet, Director, Trade Policy Research Centre, London, and it is for much helpful advice.

Preface

World War II, with the cold war as its sequel, might have been prevented if, after World War I, disarray in the West had been less widespread. Two features distinguish the present era from its predecessor. Dissarray in the West has recurred. On this occasion, however, it is both evoked and mitigated by the role that, as never before, the United States has been playing. Then, too, those who work at the highest level of world politics must pursue their quest nowadays in a more extensive context. The European balance of power has expired. A global balance, enforced by nuclear long-range weapons, is what staves off World War III.

How is the solidarity of the West to be maintained in the light of changes as stupendous as these? That which unites also divides and the first object of statecraft is to stop things from getting out of hand.

This book is no hodge-podge of essays upon unrelated issues. All matters discussed by the writer bear, directly or indirectly, upon policy for the West as it has evolved, stage by stage, since before World War II and is still evolving.

The nature of the material demands a further word. The first fifteen chapters consist of articles, dating from the late 1930s to the mid-1970s, with passages of additional comment often interspersed (in Italics). Chapter 16, written for this book and hitherto unpublished, attempts at greater length to draw some of the main threads together. Footnotes indicate whether or not articles have been pared down or slightly revised.

Finally there is the hope that a compilation which is also an analysis may be of some use. Over it all broods the spirit that John Locke expressed in his *Treatise on Government:*

> The great question which, in all ages, has disturbed mankind, and brought on them the greatest part of those

> mischiefs which have ruined cities, depopulated countries, and disordered the peace of the world, has been, not whether there be power in the world, nor whence it came, but who should have it.

This 'great question' may be decided against free societies unless they are ever alert. A turning-point is nowadays a period of time between one turning-point and another. In the West a great debate persists and if this book contributes its mite it will have served its purpose.

London, W1 Lionel Gelber

PART ONE

The European Balance Comes to an End

1 The End of the European Balance*

Hitler took office in 1933 and within a few years most of Europe trembled before him. By the middle of March 1938 when the Third Reich seized Austria, the victors of World War One lost their last chance of averting that Nazi-Soviet re-alignment which, as it lulled German fears of a war on two fronts, precipitated the Second World War. Gone, too, as events were to show, was any hope of preserving the European balance of power. After the Second World War, if free societies were to keep rivals at bay, only a global balance would do. But that, apart from global exigencies, also generates within the West itself frequent crises of its own.

Details about this essay, written during the autumn of 1937 and published by the Fortnightly *(London) during the winter of 1938, will be found in the italicised passage on page 10.*

Inside Europe a free hand for herself, outside Europe a free hand for Great Britain – this, in sum, is the substance of Germany's vision, a clue perhaps not only to what is in the front of her mind but to what may also be at the back of her policy. Now in a world progressively shorn of collective safeguards British, as well as German, calculations must at bottom be found on elements of individual and associated power. For nothing less is at stake than the European balance. It is no easy task to turn down Germany on disputed grounds of national honour or international morality alone. There is a deep-rooted feeling in Great Britain that because of the way she was handled after 1918 she must be treated with indulgence now, that, however reprehensible her conduct at

* Before this book examines some aspects of the postwar shift to a global balance, a few lasting features of wartime diplomacy are discussed in Chapter 2. Also for a sketch of prewar and wartime issues, there is a memoir, 'Anti-Nazism and a German Patriot', Chapter 7.

home and abroad, amends have yet to be made to her. No doubt the argument flies to an extreme when it condones the sinister error so fatal alike to European order and the British Commonwealth, that race, nationality and the State must be co-extensive; when, as though neither Masaryk nor Benes, Dolfuss nor Schuschnigg, had ever existed, it invokes exclusively in Germany's favour the blessed name of self-determination; and when, so irrational are the emotions aroused, the odd spectacle is furnished of Wilsonian idealism harnessed to the rule of the strong. But what has yet to be explained is why, if it be true that the *status quo* in Europe inhibits unjustly a people so virile and so dynamic as the Germans, this complaint should be applied more seldom to the Far East where, for reasons akin to their discontent with the post-war treaties, the Japanese are demonstrating how such notions work in practice.

The problem is no new one. From the days of the Tudors to those of Louis XIV, from Bonaparte to the Emperor William II, it has been a cardinal maxim of British policy to insist upon the free passage of the Narrow Seas, to keep the Low Countries out of hostile hands and to oppose the domination of Europe by any single aggressive Power or group of Powers. During the Victorian era matchless naval strength and unchallengeable industrial supremacy gave Great Britain a measure of detachment from Continental dissensions and the age-old struggle between Gaul, Teuton and Slav; to the very last Salisbury harboured what Joseph Chamberlain perceived was already obsolete, the luxury conception of the British rôle as *la puissance médiatrice.* In the twentieth century the issue was again faced squarely first by Lansdowne and then by Grey; the military superiority of Germany disturbed them before her naval aspirations widened the gulf irrevocably. Then came 1914-18, the invasion of Belgium and France, Europe in flames, the grim fulfilment of everything Lansdowne and Grey had feared and foreseen. The lesson of those years has not, however, been forgotten. In 1936 when Germany violated the Locarno Treaty Great Britain extended to Belgium and France military guarantees, exact commitments (modified and renewed a year later) which the pre-war Entente did not possess and clear testimony to her dependence in the present as in the past on the European equilibrium.

But does it suffice merely to be content with what Lord Baldwin has called our frontier on the Rhine? Is it not an illusion to think that Great Britain can withdraw securely behind Anglo-French ramparts while Germany imposes her ruthless will everywhere else in Europe? Yet beneath the attempt to induce France to drop all her Eastern commitments – which might indirectly involve Great Britain in war across the Rhine – lies the conviction that as recompense for their Western immunity the Franco-British Entente should encourage or at least assent to German ascendancy in Bohemia, Austria and beyond. Divided counsels in Great Britain are worth an army corps to Germany, and this theory has strong backing. What its adoption must entail is plain enough. Temporarily removing one peril it would create another even more deadly in the end. Accorded a free hand in Central and Eastern Europe, – and that is what the new arrangement with Austria may well mean – Germany could build a power so immense and so irresistible that in turn the West will be entirely at her mercy. The brilliant sweep of her conquests and arms from 1866 to 1918, her key-position at the heart of the continent, her interior lines of communication, her genius for organization, her national character and mentality – none of these can be left out of account. And if Sadowa preceded Sedan the interval between them was short.

Of the two barriers on Germany's south-eastward path one is less rigid than the other. Austria, moreover, is not only more vulnerable, strategically and diplomatically, than Czechoslovakia but, if she breaks under the weight brought to bear by her great neighbour from within and from without her borders, the Czechs would in any case be encircled – deserted by the disaffected section of the Sudeten minority, their further political independence automatically untenable. *Realpolitik* must turn friendships no less than enmities to account, and the main key to the gates of Vienna has hitherto reposed in Rome. On it, however, Mussolini's grip is visibly relaxing. To-day with German sympathy Italy has given such large hostages to fortune, is so impoverished by her Abyssinian and Spanish adventures, so entangled outside Central Europe with France and Great Britain, that the Italo-German agreement of 1936 about Austria has been shown to be rather a broken reed. For the famous axis is not an Italian weapon but a German bar behind which is confined the prisoner of Rome.

More almost than anything else what must influence the European balance for good or ill are the relations of Moscow with the Western Capitals. To Hitlerian diplomacy the fiction that between the ideologies of Right and Left there can be no middle way has been an undeniable asset; shielded by the anti-Communist crusade Germany has obtained latitude that would have been incredible before 1914 to pursue traditional and purely national designs of European power. Yet in determining the British attitude towards Berlin and Moscow alike the governing factor can no longer be political theory or moral judgment but the map of Europe; geography has decreed, and history teaches, that the rise of an ambitious, eruptive Power nearby is an immeasurably greater hazard to the British Isles than the machinations of one that is both more self-contained and more remote. By every dispassionate calculation of power-politics if Russia and the Anglo-French Entente have similar interests in Central and Eastern Europe they may, in a spirit not of mutual esteem but of common exigency, be expected to stand together. What Moscow no less than London has to decide is whether, granting that they possess such interests, they are disposed again to collaborate in their support.

Russia's pacts of non-aggression, her entry into the League of Nations and her treaties of mutual assistance with France and Czechoslovakia were a natural response to the demagogic rattle of the Hitlerian sabre. By some English champions of the new *Drang nach Osten* Russo-German tension has been regarded as not altogether unfortunate; if the Soviet and the Third Reich were embroiled against each other the rest of Europe might breathe more freely. But the plain fact is that before Germany could make inroads in southern Russia or annex the Ukraine the whole of Central and Eastern Europe must come into her grasp; and if that happened the German shadow would lie as heavily over the West as over the East. And what if Russia herself suffers a change of heart? Noting sardonically the triumphs of Italo-German diplomacy in the Abyssinian, Locarno and Spanish controversies she may wonder whether she will not be left by the Western Powers with most of the burden of stemming the eastward Nazi tide; whether – the remilitarization of the Rhineland being here a critical point – without them it is one she can or should bear; whether in such a case antagonism even to Hitler is really worth her while. And should Russia, sceptical of the value of further co-operation with Great Britain and France (although it has contributed weightily to the European balance and therefore to her own advantage), now conclude that her best line of defence is, after all, her own frontier, would not the German task be enormously simplified?

Where bluster fails smoother accents may succeed. Divested of its ideological trappings, Hitler's truculent effort to expel Russia from the councils of Europe is an endeavour to isolate her so as to hamstring collective security, impair the French system, weaken Czechoslovakia and set in train that mastery of the Danubian basin which must be the foundation of his continental power. But may not events in the Far East slowly evoke a drastic revision of policy? So long as there was a prospect of simultaneous Japanese pressure on Asiatic Russia some Nazis could toy with grandiose projects of taking in their stride along with the smaller Eastern States the outer fringes of the Soviet – although British neutrality and the use of Polish soil for the German legions might also have been essential. But to these plans does not Japan's large-scale war in China constitute a rebuff as shattering as it was unexpected? For the more her blood and treasure are poured out below the Great Wall the lower must sink her stock in any well-timed anti-Russian enterprise. Thus Russia, despite the execution of Tukhachevsky and his colleagues, despite the loss of her most talented military leaders – and the closer unity of the high command with the *régime* may in itself be adequate compensation – is much more secure than she was a year ago; the threat of a joint German-Japanese onslaught correspondingly less real. And, for the moment, in this sense, too, China's anguish is to some extent the price of Europe's peace. But must Germany forswear her cherished aims altogether because Japan has embarked on war in the cause of Japanese rather than German expansion? A military understanding with Tokio being ruled out, would not a political understanding with Moscow serve her more limited purposes better?

The *Reichswehr* at least may think so and (Ministerial predilections notwithstanding) they have still a great part to play. Certainly it would enable them to deal with Poland as they had originally intended or with less danger of paralysing interference turn at once south-eastward where much awaits them before Russian soil is even touched. On the Rapallo policy they have always looked with favour, and the treaty which Germany first signed with Russia in 1922 was not only renewed in 1933 by Hitler himself but in spite of the subsequent anti-Soviet campaign has never been denounced. The *Reichswehr* and the Red Army have a long record of fellowship, while German capitalists might again desire opportunities they previously enjoyed in developing Soviet industry. Whatever the ideological pretext, Hitler has tried to sever the tie between Russia, Czechoslovakia, France and the League of Nations for strategic reasons with which every German statesman since Bismarck has been painfully familiar; the West not being intimidated by the *furor teutonicus* and the wire to the Kremlin having never irreparably been cut he may undertake to gain his ends at Moscow itself. And neither for the Soviet nor for the Third Reich would that mean a more startling metamorphosis in foreign policy than others they have undergone; before Hitler's pact with Pilsudski the relations of Germany with Poland seemed as irremediably bad as they now do with Russia. Since Bismarck's day Germany has always strengthened the chain of her own 'encirclement'; if she jettisons her policy of encircling the Soviet she may break a link which she forged against herself. With Japan engrossed more than ever in China and with Italy's gaze fixed overseas it is the Western Powers rather than Moscow who have most to yield to the so-called counter-league of Rome, Berlin and Tokio. In China and Central Europe alike the ultimate political and economic interests of Germany are not those of her present associates; by a union of forces she must help them – as they must help her – to extort from Great Britain and France more than they could each have procured alone in order to offset discrepancies which render their combination fundamentally so unstable. A fit alignment for power-diplomacy at London and Paris, the impermanent triangular coalition is not an insuperable obstacle between Berlin and Moscow.

What then British opinion must appreciate is that Russia dwells under no inescapable obligation to support the European balance. Even now it is not improbable that her reawakening nationalism, with an eye to the enemies by whom she is encompassed, can in some degree be traced to disappointment at the poor fruits of collaboration with Western internationalism. And if Hitler provoked the emergence of Soviet diplomacy from its comparative seclusion he also can purchase its retirement to something like its former state.

In these circumstances the British objective should be clear. The European equipoise to be maintained at all must be steady at both ends. It is the policy of the British Government to circumvent ideological groupings, to work irrespective of internal *régimes* with every Power bent upon peace; and what is sauce for the German goose is sauce for the Russian gander. For by repudiating the League of Nations the Rome – Berlin – Tokyo camp have created that which Great Britain seeks to dispel; between Russia and the West, however, so long as she is represented at Geneva, the machinery for co-operation remains. The Soviet may still prefer to avoid dependence on German goodwill, and it would be a blunder of the first magnitude if Anglo-French diplomacy allowed that preference to wither in exasperation and despair. To emasculate the Covenant so that Russia as well as the smaller Eastern States could rely no longer on any form of collective security may be further to push them one by one into Hitler's arms; and if the Soviet pacts with France and Czechoslovakia were deprived of all substance the process would only be accelerated. Just as Grey and his contemporaries, beset with the overweening pretensions of Germany, could not afford to perpetuate Anglo-Russian misunderstanding, so neither can the British Government to-day. There is no question of a fastidious choice between rival creeds or of deciding whether or not the Soviet tyranny outstrips the worst iniquities of the Tsardom. In every way save one Great Britain and Germany had more in common before the War than Great Britain and Russia; in every way save one the same may even be true again. But that one exception was and is crucial. The disappearance from European politics of the Russian counterpoise would mean that the Third Reich had achieved a goal for which Imperial Germany strove in vain. So dire a setback, unless the balance of power has lost its importance for Great Britain, unless geography is a snare and history a delusion, it is now the business of British statesmanship to do what it can to prevent.

When the English-speaking peoples spurned any such argument, humanity was to pay a heavy toll. This analysis, reproduced here in full, first appeared as 'Britain and the European Balance' in the Fortnightly *(London, 1 March 1938). It was thus published two weeks before the Germans entered Austria, six months before Munich, a year before the Nazis marched into Prague, more than a year and a half before Stalin let Hitler temporarily buy him off.*

The Nazi-Soviet Pact was signed on 23 August 1939. Not until the late spring and early summer of that year did European chancellories hear rumours of an impending Russo-German turnabout. In his memoirs Charles Bohlen tells how, from 20 May 1939, the Moscow Embassy of the United States was relaying to the State Department information he was getting from a German anti-Nazi official, Johnny Herwarth. After World War II the latter explained to Bohlen that he felt early disclosure of the coming Russo-German agreement would stave off conflict. There was actually no such disclosure. Cordell Hull, the Secretary of State, took London and Paris into his confidence only when the Nazi-Soviet Pact had been completed. Nor does what it entailed seem to have been fully appreciated in official quarters. But this should have long been evident.*

*Charles E. Bohlen, *Witness to History, 1929-1969* (W. W. Norton & Co, Inc., New York, N.Y., 1973) pp. 67-87.

'If disclosed at any earlier date,' writes one historian, 'it might have frustrated a German-Soviet pact. It would have forced a triple alliance at whatever price the U.S.S.R. demanded. It would also have deflated Neville Chamberlain's confidence that Europe's two most bitterly opposed dictatorships could never ally.' Sidney Aster, *1939 The Making of a Second World War* (Andre Deutsch Ltd, London, 1973) p. 316.

If there is no Russian withdrawal and the French system does not wholly dissolve, Czechoslovakia may face the future with renewed confidence. As for Austria, the weakest of the dykes against the surging German flood, her fate is necessarily influenced by British relations with yet another Great Power. Of that point indeed Mr Baldwin's Government seem, during the Italo-Ethiopian crisis, to have been fully aware; it looks like being the trump card up Mussolini's sleeve at present. For the vindication of the Covenant in 1935, even if collectively feasible, might not only have hastened the collapse of Italy but also – with the relics of the League providing a battered trophy for a further Hitlerian triumph – have expedited the surrender to Germany of Central Europe. Ironic as it may now appear the fact is that on the European continent Great Britain and Italy are natural allies. Signor Mussolini must know perfectly well that his vigil on the Brenner is an Anglo-French interest which cannot endure if his *régime* crumbles and chaos ensues; the British, on the other hand, knowing equally well that he dare not forfeit Italy's European position, refuse to pay him for what is, after all, his primary duty to his own country. It is a trial of strength, one in which, if unduly prolonged, neither of the contestants but Hitler will be the winner. A fillip to his prestige, concrete advantages to embody it – these are Mussolini's immediate requirements. For, unless he is soon to find himself in complete vassalage to Berlin with scarcely equivalent gains elsewhere, a settlement from Great Britain and France must be extracted at an early date.

If there is a Franco-British deal with Italy what becomes of the Covenant, the rule of law, the decencies of international life? Perhaps it is no mere question of letting justice be done, though the Mediterranean heavens fall. For Geneva to insist unavailingly upon the restoration of one primitive African State may be to fail while yet there is time to preserve the freedom of others in Europe itself. Will conscience be salved, the decencies of international life upheld, will the Covenant, the rule of law be in a healthier condition when most of Central and Eastern Europe is converted into a German province? And, even from an ideological point of view, it must be accounted a feeble victory for democracy if Fascism gives way simply to enhance Nazi predominance. For here is no clean-cut decision between right and wrong but a choice of the lesser evil. There are those who distinguish between a British policy founded on the Covenant and one guided by the principle of the balance of power. Whether or not the contrast was once valid it is in the circumstances of to-day a false antithesis, a total misconception of the necessities of the case. Only by maintaining the balance of power can Great Britain and France support a European order in which the ideals of the League may somehow linger and in some happier hour even flourish again. If the equilibrium is demolished, the League goes irretrievably and much else besides.

Conducted with prudence and skill British diplomacy may yet steer mankind away from disaster. Ceaselessly and impressively the mounting armaments and deepening friendships of Great Britain tend to repair her damaged authority. That, despite the high-flown insolence of Japan in the Far East, matters nearer home come first, the concentration of the fleet in and about European waters abundantly indicates. Nor are further continental commitments, of which public opinion might not approve, wholly indispensable. In the present situation uncertainty about British intentions may serve as a deterrent to German expansion only less effective than formal but impracticable iron-clad guarantees. There are circumstances in which imprecision is the bane of international negotiation; there can be circumstances in which it may prove a tower of strength. The mere fact that Hitler has always sought an understanding with Great Britain, of which the premise would be that she disinterest herself in Central and Eastern Europe, shows that unless he gets it he is afraid to move. So long as Great Britain withholds her consent to a free hand, there will be a haunting dread at Berlin that she may in any ultimate crisis intervene. And if Germany remembers the kind of mistake about Great Britain that was made in 1914, the indefinite, the unpredictable nature of the British attitude in an emergency should keep alive in German calculations a saving anxiety not to repeat it.

Herr Hitler, may of course, take a chance on the British love of peace. The danger will be intensified if important sections of the public mind in Great Britain, by finding excuses for him in advance, incite him, as they often do, to some reckless action; if, too, at critical junctures Ministers themselves hamper their own diplomatic influence by saying gratuitously that they will not run the risk of war. It may be so, but why say it? A studied vagueness which will keep Hitler guessing cannot add to the perils confronting Central and Eastern Europe; it might, the potential threat of British participation being what it is, keep them in abeyance. The special Entente problem of July – August, 1914, will not again arise – not, at any rate, in the same shape; the Anglo-French military guarantees of 1936-37 are explicit and comprehensive. But the people and Parliament of Great Britain still retain the liberty to decide on the merits of each case elsewhere in Europe as it occurs. To barter away that liberty might be to bring about the very predicament that it must be the supreme object of British policy avert.

Nor will the growth of English-speaking solidarity – sympathy with Great Britain in the Dominions and the United States alike – have a negligible effect on the chancelleries of Europe. Experience indeed should warn Berlin that here, too, is another unknown quantity with which it would be foolhardy not to reckon. For much that has happened since the Treaty of Versailles, Great Britain and the United States are apt to blame each other; in any final crisis what draws them closer is a view of human society which transcends every difference, however pronounced, of outlook, geography and tradition. And Great Britain must make the most of this fact even though, in the absence of continuous collaboration such as is feasible with France, British policy may of necessity resort to disillusioning compromises. Properly understood it is a vital interest of the United States, as of the British Commonwealth as a whole, that Great Britain should be able to maintain the European equilibrium, for with it is bound up not only her own security and independence but the distribution of power all the world over.

After the outbreak of war, two events saved the West. There was, first of all, Hitler's attack on his former Russian confederate in June 1941. There was, secondly, Pearl Harbour in December 1941 when the Japanese, Axis allies of the

Third Reich, assailed the American Pacific Fleet and so put the United States fully at the side of Britain. How American isolationism might be surmounted could not be foreseen when, before the fall of Austria, this essay was first published. That it would be surmounted was undoubted if, as a favourable distribution of European power was bound up with American security, the United States could not let Britain fall. After World War II, however, no European balance could be restored. When the cold war began a global balance took over.

At a time of profound disquiet it is a heartening sign of their faith and temper that in free countries on both sides of the Atlantic so many voices should clamour for a common ideological front dedicated to the defence of democracy; a programme which contemplates improved relations with the Russian and Italian dictatorships, if not utterly repugnant, assuredly must exercise less popular appeal. To buttress the continental balance may none the less be the sole means of upholding an international order in which the democratic institutions of both Western Europe and the New World can safely survive to await the dawn of a better day. For what the morrow will bring no man can tell, but if the unity of the English-speaking peoples stands unshaken and infuses into the diplomacy of peace reserves of strength as vast as they are undefined, the politics of war may yet be overawed.

2 The Wartime Origins of Some Major Postwar Issues*

As the date was set at the Teheran Conference for a West European or second front to be opened by Britain and the United States, that conclave probably marked the apex of wartime good feeling between Russia and the West. It was after the Big Three met again at Yalta, in February 1945, that Churchill began to fear, an apprehension shared by Roosevelt before his death, how Stalin might violate agreements reached about the postwar frontiers of Poland and about the principle of self-determination for the countries of Eastern Europe once victory over Hitler had been won. But at Teheran there were, as yet, no definite glimmerings of that cold war which cropped up during the final wartime meeting of the victor Great Powers at Potsdam in July 1945 and before the war in the Pacific had been terminated.

This essay, written while the Nazi assault on the Soviet Union was diverting the Germans from pounding harder on Britain and published in the spring of 1944, dealt therefore more uncritically with Russian designs than the essay which preceded it and those that follow.

Account should also be taken of the cordial atmosphere at Teheran by such revisionist historians as have accused the West of the main responsibility for the cold war. After World War II, as after World War I, a self-hating Western school of thought again overlooked what the stakes of power had become.

When the Great Powers met in the autumn of 1943, they are reported to have conferred over broad objectives rather than exact detail. Nevertheless, enough has been made known

*This essay, with some passages removed, was first published as an article, 'With Power to Preserve the Peace', in the *Virginia Quarterly Review* (Charlottesville, Virginia, Spring 1944), soon after the Big Three met at Teheran.

of their deliberations to furnish a fairly coherent pattern of the postwar order. By some who have praised those transactions, and by observers such as Mr Wendell Willkie, this is not quite appreciated. If they had examined the work of Moscow, Cairo, and Teheran as a whole and not in part, they might have dissented from a philosophy of international relations which until now has been under attack but which the world's foremost statesmen have had the wisdom to espouse.

For the wartime unity achieved and the peacetime unity promised, there has been natural acclaim. What did cause alarm was the fear that the Great Powers might still pursue their labours *à trois* or *à quatre* rather than by wider meetings. The means employed is, however, inseparable from the things accomplished. Mr Churchill and Mr Roosevelt signed the Atlantic Charter, and the United Nations, by the very act which brought them together, subsequently endorsed it. First dual and then universal, this method of framing objectives was too narrow at the outset and afterwards too broad to be effectual. It had to be corrected and it was when, with the entry of Russia into partnership with Britain and the United States, a Concert of victor Great Powers came into being. Collaborating as a single unit, the United Nations might lay down general principles. It is too unwieldy in size and its constituents too diverse in strength to do much else. Britain and the United States might, on the other hand, define the aims they cherish for Europe; they would, without the concurrence of Russia, be beating in the air. And it is this that gives the declarations of Moscow and Teheran the breath of life. For here are principles which are neither too general in conception – though general principles are imperative – nor too limited in sponsorship. The power combine which is chiefly winning the war has resolved to have the main voice in the enforcement of the peace.

Does that signify they are going to dictate the world settlement? This they were afterwards at pains to deny. A statement by the Moscow Conference on that score (November 1, 1943) provoked apprehensions which a further statement at Teheran (December 1, 1943) may have been designed to quiet. But the first of these pronouncements did not cancel out the second; it explained more fully the intentions of

Britain, the United States, and Russia, but it did not alter their plan of procedure. For what they said at Moscow was that 'pending the establishment of law and order and the inauguration of a system of general security, they will consult with one another and *as occasion requires* with other members of the United Nations with a view to joint action on behalf of the community of nations'. The period of transition may be a long one. During it the great triumvirate, save as pressure is exerted on them by others, will themselves be judges of the 'occasions' which call for more extended consultations. As trustees of the peace, Britain, the United States, and Russia will, in short, not hold everything up until all heads are counted and the vote of every minor State has been registered. In no other manner can delays be overcome and chaos averted. The responsibility of leadership resting on the victor Great Powers, they propose to exercise it and to exercise it together.

This was a wartime expedient. Within the North Atlantic Alliance it remains a serious irritant and during the early 1970s France in particular raged against a Russo-American detente as a condominium of the two super-powers.

When this prospect evoked protests, the three statesmen of Teheran withdrew nothing but approached the question on another plane. Where Mr Eden, Mr Molotov, and Mr Hull had been more concerned at Moscow with the short run, Mr Churchill, Mr Stalin, and Mr Roosevelt stressed the long run. For what Teheran did in this respect was not to discard the Moscow technique, but to suggest the circumstances which would render even enemy countries eligible later on for more extended consultations. The peace envisaged is, they declared, one which will command goodwill from the 'overwhelming' masses of the peoples of the world; and the fact that it may not appeal to all but only to an 'overwhelming' number deserves attention. For it is beyond the wit of man to devise a settlement which everyone will gladly accept. Germany, for instance, waged an insidious campaign after 1919 to revise the Versailles Treaty and the sympathy she aroused in the Western world caused us to lower our own defences. Her underlying grievance was, nevertheless, not against particular injustices but at rock-bottom against the loss of the war itself. To reverse the verdict of 1914-18 was her goal – one she almost reached in 1940. And that is why concessions to her always were so fruitless; only by letting ourselves be vanquished and herself victorious could Germany be made content. History, which has been repeating itself through two German wars with the utmost violence, may tend also to repeat itself after the next settlement is imposed. To watch against that, to have peace prevail against the warlike minority among nations, the peace-loving majority are banding themselves together. But if there is proof of good faith from Germans, Japanese, or other aggressors, should they ever undergo a thorough transformation, they, too, can and ought to join.

This principle could be applied only to those beyond the reach of Soviet tentacles. It embraced an ex-enemy like Italy but not such anti-German countries as Czechoslovakia, Poland and, with the delicate exception of Finland, others in the Soviet imperium. Austria perforce afterwards had to observe a traditional brand of neutrality. India, a former dependency of Britain's and still a member of the Commonwealth, became by her own volition the foremost exponent of Third World neutralism. China signed up with Russia first but is now less hostile towards the West than towards her.

At Teheran the three Great Powers did not abate the purpose they had disclosed at Moscow to lead the new system of peace; they merely clarified its extent: 'We shall seek the co-operation and active participation of all nations, large and small, whose peoples in heart and mind are dedicated, as are our own peoples, to the elimination of tyranny and slavery, oppression and intolerance. We will welcome them as they may choose to come into the world family of democratic nations.' But what if they do not all choose to come into the world family of democratic nations? Then to back the peace of those who do so choose, there will be a preponderance of power.

These were objectives to which, as in the Atlantic Charter of 14 August 1941, Franklin Delano Roosevelt and Winston

Churchill could again subscribe without reserve. Even Stalin, like his less bloodthirsty political heirs, might regard Communist dictatorship as a legitimate branch of people's democracy. But what could have passed through the mind of each signatory when they proclaimed at Teheran that all of them presided over systems dedicated to the elimination of tyranny and slavery, oppression and intolerance?

On this each of the United Nations might see eye to eye. But at a continuous initiative from the Great Powers they may still demur. Yet wherever any country, minor, intermediate, or major, has a special function to discharge, its rôle, large or small, ought to be gauged by the value of the part it can play. At Cairo, Mr Churchill and Mr Roosevelt decided with Generalissimo Chiang Kai-shek that the possessions of China will be returned to her, Korea set free, and Japan shorn of everything she has gained by conquest since the end of the nineteenth century. Prior to that the Chinese representative, while not contributing more directly to the tripartite conference at Moscow, had signed the Four-Nation Declaration on peace and security after the war. But can China provide the same weight of leadership in international affairs as the others? That is improbable. The time was ripe, however, to pledge her the reward she has richly earned, to dispel war-weariness, and to furnish an incentive for her to persevere in tying up Japanese armies on the Asiatic mainland until the West, less preoccupied with the conflict in Europe, can concentrate on the Far Eastern struggle. It will, as a matter of fact, be many years before China might hope to summon the power which would enable her to do a proportionate share with Britain, Russia, and the United States on what must virtually be the steering committee of the postwar world. As a modern State she is politically underorganized and economically undeveloped; her finances are wildly inflated. Pacification not so much abroad as at home will be her task after many years of civil no less than foreign strife. The circle drawn at Moscow, Teheran, and Cairo is, after all, not a closed one. Despite the pessimism of Field Marshal Smuts about the recovery of France, history and necessity alike bear witness that, sooner or later, it is her chair at the centre table which must and will be filled.

By 1950 it had become the condition of detente with Maoist China that undertakings signed at Cairo on the eve of the Teheran Conference should still be honoured.

As for the recovery of France, not even the French people were united over this during the autumn of 1943.

Does the past demonstrate that a concert of Great Powers is always unstable and prone to collapse? After 1919 a more collective system, without such an inner grouping, was of shorter duration than the one, much recast since 1815, which preceded it. What we now must have is a blend of constructive elements from the two; a world Concert of victor Great Powers should be to the United Nations as the spinal cord is to the human body. For when the Great Powers have stood and will stand together – as long, that is, as they have a sufficient community of interest – any system of peace can succeed; when they each go their own way, or abstain, it must fail. Major wars occur when major countries are embroiled; they can be prevented only when Great Powers are prepared in unison to restrain them. The fact that during the nineteen thirties the lesser Powers did not stop aggressors showed that they could not. For at Geneva, whether in crises of the peace or on other issues before the League of Nations, it was frequently the minor and middle Powers who expressed the conscience of mankind. That right without might may be impotent is what those tragic, those wasted years have taught. And it would be the bitterest of all paradoxes if, just at the moment when the Great Powers realized this brutal truth, the other nations were to forget it. Prospering by our divisions, Germany again took up arms, not because her adversaries among the Great Powers did too much, but because, either by being at variance with each other or by holding themselves aloof, they did too little.

Peace by power is, then, no monopoly of power for its own sake. What it does demand is a preponderance or favourable balance of power efficiently regulated and managed to reinforce the wider system of peace. Collective security after Versailles was neither collective nor secure. There is now a chance, with a new Concert of the victor Great Powers at the head of the United Nations, that it will be both. At the

Moscow Conference it was recognized that there would have to be established 'a general international organization based on the principle of the sovereign equality of all peace-loving States, and open to membership by all such States, large and small, for the maintenance of international peace and security'. Since Britain from the outset, and Russia toward the last, belonged to the League of Nations, their policy in this regard is less novel than that of the United States. As recently as August, 1941, when he signed the Atlantic Charter, Mr Roosevelt could not be as definite – so palpable is the change in American opinion during the two years that the United States has been at war. And this is exemplified by the resolution which the American Senate passed (November 15, 1943) as soon as the Moscow Conference had adjourned. For their resolution not only incorporated some of the identical phrases of the Moscow Declaration; it went further and deeper when it called for an international authority 'with power to prevent aggression and to preserve the peace of the world'. An authority of that kind and with that sort of power would be one with teeth in it. The Senate's language strikes at the root of our troubles.* But will it display the same insight when, as in 1919-20, it has before it once more the final documents of a peace settlement or settlements to ratify or reject? For the showdown will come when the victor Powers can be accused of underwriting treaties of which irate pressure groups may disapprove or against which interested parties, foreign and domestic, might either stir up fresh storms of American isolationism or at least compel some curtailment of participation by the United States in the affairs of Europe. Until boundaries are demarcated, economic arrangements framed, the international authority in motion, the danger zone, so far as the Senate and American opinion are concerned, has still to be crossed.

It is for this reason, if for no other, that terms such as the grand alliance, or nuclear alliance, to describe the accord reached in Moscow, Cairo, and Teheran, should be avoided. A

*There had been a survey of these troubles in the present writer's book, *Peace By Power* (Oxford University Press, New York, London, Toronto, 1942).

world Concert of the victor Great Powers does, fortunately, now exist; only between two of them, Britain and Russia, are there legal commitments. A Grand Alliance in which reciprocal guarantees are adopted might be what fundamentally the new international authority will constitute. It has yet to be set up. Meanwhile a Grand Alliance, limited to Europe, may be taking shape. With the twenty-year Anglo-Russian Alliance of 1942 to maintain against Germany a preponderating balance of power might be linked the similar Russo-Czech Alliance of 1943. Consisting of mutual defensive obligations and having a precise strategic object, this can be the core of a European Grand Alliance to which France and most liberated nations may be expected to adhere. Should the United States and other non-European countries accept military guarantees of Europe's peace, a strictly European coalition will be less urgent. When concluded, it was perceived that the Anglo-Russian treaty might merge into a larger system of security to preserve the fruits of victory. But if American commitments in Europe are partial, semi-detached, or principally economic, Europe's own Grand Alliance will be the foundation of power on which in the first resort her peace and safety must repose.

This is not to underestimate the mission of the looser Concert of victor Great Powers. Through it the United States can join her other partners in hammering out the treatment of European and Asiatic problems – even if her political obligations in Europe are to be less than theirs. As the two German wars indicate, she needs their European predominance as much as they need her support. It is possible that the international authority will come forth with adequate power and with complete American participation. But unless it does, there may have to be room within it for a protective coalition purely European in scope.

As late as Teheran it was thus supposed that, with support from Russia, the European balance of power could still be restored. Some years later when, with the United States and Canada as co-signatories, the North Atlantic Alliance had been signed, it was against Russia herself that 'a protective coalition' had to be directed.

At Moscow and at Teheran the accent was on democracy – at Moscow on Italian democracy, at Teheran on a world family of democratic nations. And if it be asked of Russia, as a champion of democracy, whether Saul also is among the prophets, the answer is plain. As the Soviet Constitution is applied, there will be less to distinguish Russia from those States, with a different economy, in which representative government is practised and safeguards are enacted for the liberty of the subject. From their doctrines, despite the Nazi-Soviet pact and the persistence of earlier connections, it is hardly surprising that the One-Party State of Communism should be at death's grip with the One-Party State of National Socialism; the vehicles resembled each other, but not the purposes served. The issue, in any case, while reflecting the clash of ideologies, transcends it. For the patriots of the Kremlin have seldom been wedded to doctrine at the expense of country; that is a luxury in which only foreign Communists could afford to indulge. The one solid rock of policy is national interest. Britain, Russia, and the United States are in concert because collaboration between them is accomplishing for each what each cannot accomplish by itself alone. First victory and then a settlement in which victory will be inviolate is what they seek in common and what none can attain until, Italian Fascism having been crushed, it is followed by the downfall of Japanese militarism and of that political heritage of a greater Germany of which Nazism is but one contemporary phase. Whether democracy, the antithesis of these doctrines, will be workable in areas where it has never worked before, only the future can tell. But to promote it is to foster pacific trends and on that we all can take our stand.

Yet while the Great Powers may attribute virtue to democracy, do they condemn nationalism as evil? Against national sovereignty there has been clamour for a federalist remedy of the world's ills. But at Moscow they declared for a general international organization based on 'the *sovereign* equality of all peace-loving States'. A blow to federalist schemes, it was nevertheless inevitable. That does not preclude federal experiments of a more limited character, one of which is exemplified in the grant of national autonomy in military and foreign affairs (February 1944) to the United Republics of the Soviet Union. The emphasis there, however, is not on federalism as a single mould in which all Europe will be recast but on federalism as a regional instrument of Russian national policy – and with a consequent stress on nationality itself. This is not to justify the national self-worship of Germans or Japanese; their primitive frenzies, the power of the victors and the new international authority must curb at all costs. But for the postwar world a twofold process is emerging. We are to witness the leadership of the Great Powers and yet they in turn have affirmed their own respect for the national rights of others. If the principle of democracy is vindicated within countries, it cannot, after all, be overridden between them. For democracy and leadership are not antagonistic. Leadership without democracy, between as within States, spells dictatorship; but democracy without leadership, between as within States, invites anarchy. Primarily, each of the United Nations, large and small, is fighting for its own national freedom. But what if two nationalisms arrayed against the same enemy are themselves in conflict? We may acknowledge the validity of the national impulse without acquiescing in its maximum claims. An extreme internationalism as set forth in federalist blueprints has obviously been impracticable from the start – history was not only against it, and the nature of world politics, but the art of government and the varied national aspirations of the embattled peoples. Yet a nationalism which goes to the opposite extreme is a perpetual incitement to war. The prerequisite for the self-determination of lesser European States is a good understanding between the larger ones. They cannot poison relations between Great Powers without themselves suffering most. To reconcile a moderate nationalism with a sane internationalism will still be, as the years unfold, one of the central tasks of statesmanship.

And it is in the same pragmatic manner that the vexed problem of imperialism will have to be adjusted to the strivings of peoples less able to stand together or to stand at all on their own feet. At a time when the United States has been precipitated into war by an assault on some of her colonies and outposts, when Russia in Europe and Asia is bound to retain the vast territories to which her sway during the past century has extended, there is still the delusion that in contrast to Britain they are immaculately anti-imperialist. But the campaign for the liquidation of the British Empire is subsiding as Russia further consolidates her own empire and the United States, peering at the Japanese-mandated islands, glancing perhaps towards other points of the compass, considers another expansion of her oceanic realm. It is curious, therefore, to hear those who have been critical of the imperial foundations of Britain's European and world power utter the complaint that at the Cairo Conference 'nothing was said about how America would get the bases she needs in the Pacific in order to feel secure'. Between their meetings at Moscow, Cairo, and Teheran the Great Powers could not have been, and unofficial disclosures intimate that they were not, so remiss. For if their Concert is to continue, they must appraise the secret not only of their own safety and strategic effectiveness, but of each other's.

How much the Big Three were in accord at their 1943 Conferences may be deduced from Russia's acceptance at Moscow of the Anglo-American terms, as drafted at Casablanca, for unconditional surrender and of the further plan, asserted at Teheran, for the destruction of the German forces. Before this there had been anxiety over the flirtation of the Soviet Government with their puppet 'Free German' committee. For the *tour de valse* which Russia undertook with German reactionary elements, as well as Marxians and liberals, implied that she would be willing to treat for peace on a basis of something less than unconditional surrender or the obliteration of German military strength. As a satellite of Russia, a so-called German 'democracy' might conceal a military potential which would prove useful in the event of the other Great Powers being hostile to the Soviet. If Soviet diplomacy had been hinting at a Russo-German grouping, that dire historic alternative to collaboration with the West, any such gestures ceased at Moscow and Teheran. For one thing, the Russians discovered that Britain would not resist their Polish policy. Perhaps the story will be similar over Russian intentions elsewhere on the Baltic and in the Balkans. There must also have been agreement over questions raised at Moscow, Cairo, and Teheran touching the empire of the Soviet in the Far East. For if Russia were not going to get what is substantially her own way in these matters, her dissatisfaction with the Conferences would have been quickly felt.

The impression that there will be no maudlin settlement with the foe was deepened when Mr Roosevelt spoke at Christmas, 1943, on 'peace by force' and said that at Teheran they concurred 'that Germany must be stripped of her military might and be given no opportunity within the foreseeable future to regain that might'. Sauce for the Japanese goose is sauce for the German gander; one policy could not be adopted at Cairo towards Japan and another adopted at Moscow and Teheran towards Germany. This should be noted, for there is a school of thought which would be lenient with Germany while severe with Japan. The latter, after all, has in our midst no troop of exiled intellectuals, still Japanese at heart, who in books and articles might agitate on behalf of the 'better' Japan; she possessed even less than Germany's ineffectual, weak-kneed liberalism on which we are again being exhorted to rely; yet her record without it has in the past hundred years been no worse.

That the Chancelleries of the Concert have a more responsible outlook may also be discerned in the Moscow declaration on the independence of Austria. For this not only illustrated that, in their attitude towards Germany, they had drawn the right conclusions from the history of the nineteenth and twentieth centuries; it was also a classic example in world politics of the ineradicable function of power. Ever since the Hapsburg domains fell apart there had, on grounds of 'race,' language, and economics, been a case for the union of Austria and Germany. But more compelling than these is the strategy of freedom, and to conform with it that union will be undone. From 1919 to Munich it was evident that Czechoslovakia could not withstand the Teutonic encirclement which the absorption of Austria by Germany entailed. The resurrection of Austria and the redemption of Czechoslovakia thus coincide. And the servitude of Europe will end where it began.

It was, then, as a clue to the security of Europe and therefore to the peace of the world that the Austrian problem may have been singled out at Moscow for special mention. Germany's conquest of Austria, furnishing her with the control of Eastern Europe and the mastery of the continent, constituted a drastic shift in the balance of power. Now, as the balance of power mounts adversely against her, Germany's dominance toppling, Europe will be liberated. That is why, when the three Great Powers announced at Moscow that Austria would be cut off from Germany, they were in fact declaring that a greater Germany, regardless of her political complexion, can never again be tolerated. This, moreover, is the policy which the Anglo-Russian and Czech-Soviet twenty-year alliances are calculated to underpin. For the victors are going to redress by their own preponderance that balance of power which they had piled up to their credit in 1919, which in a mania of suicide they flung away after 1933, and which they are about to retrieve.

The further concrete application of this principle is not yet known. But what is good for Austria – the fundamental rule of a weaker Germany having been promulgated – may be good for other historic German States. The industrial war potential and military striking-power of the present Reich are enhanced and facilitated by its territorial integrity and political unity, both of which, in their modern form, date only from 1871 and neither of which is sacrosanct. For disunification between Germanic States is not the same as dismemberment by foreign countries. But Russia, decentralizing her own government, might boggle at neither. 'We cannot end the war,' said M. Molotov to the Supreme Soviet on February 1, 1944, 'by the military defeat of Germany alone. It must end with the moral and political annihilation of Germany.' Having urged Poland to consent to the Curzon line frontier, Russia wishes Poland to be compensated with lands under German rule – with East Prussia, if not Silesia and Pomerania –, easier access to the sea being accompanied presumably by a transfer of populations. One thing is clear. By making or acquiescing in a compromise of that sort, the Powers will have admitted that the national and territorial contours of the Bismarckian Reich may be altered. The vanquished having yielded, the victors might refuse to recognize any centralized régime in Berlin and insist on negotiating separately with several or more Germanic sovereignties in their ancient State capitals. Better economic treatment could be offered each of the Germanies in the years to come than they can possibly get as a formidable single unit – provided they fulfil the prime condition of genuine independence from each other. To guard against their reunion might be costly. It would be less costly, and more swiftly acted on, than the exhausting vigilance imposed by the constant spectre – even if, for the moment, it be democratic and pacific in guise – of a unified, greater Germany.

The Soviet advance into Central Europe did not decentralise the German Reich, Bismarck's masterpiece, but, with the advent of the cold war, split it in two.

The partition or reunification of Germany became a key issue of the cold war. Time alone will tell how close to a solution was the Ostpolitik *of Herr Willy Brandt – from which the detente policies of Messrs Nixon and Kissinger took off.**

It has still to be seen whether steps such as these are as feasible as they are desirable. But they are in thorough consonance with that triumph of realism over sentimentality which Moscow and Teheran symbolized. A month before President Roosevelt spoke (Christmas, 1943) of 'peace by force,' Field Marshal Smuts had stated that the question of power is the great lesson of this war: 'Peace unbacked by power remains a dream.' It is well that these grim truths should be enunciated at last in the highest quarters. Until of late, it was heresy to advocate peace by power; to argue that a liberated Europe must rest on the balance of power held in the hands of the victors; that on their sleepless preponder-

*The case for dividing the German Reich into its historic components was discussed by the present writer in *Peace By Power*, pp. 30-5 and 88-102 of the American and Canadian editions. Along the lines of the postwar Marshall Plan, the need for the economic rehabilitation of European countries, including the German states, was also recognised, ibid., pp. 27-8. These proposals preceded the more punitive Morgenthau Plan by two years.

ance and on it alone can be established a collective authority to maintain peace. Even Mr Cordell Hull, on his return from the Moscow Conference, remarked that its labours had the effect of superseding the balance of power, when in fact that preponderance, in diplomacy if not yet by arms, had just been renewed. For the balance of power is not a precarious equipoise keeping equals at bay, but a scales on which one side or the other swings to the top. It is embodied in an ascendancy of the peace-loving nations over an historic war-maker, and it will decline if that historic warmaker is permitted to conserve again the mainsprings of his strength.

Since Napoleon there have been two major treaty settlements – that at Vienna in 1815 and that at Paris in 1919 – when the victors seemed to have within their grasp a world which might be shaped anew. And now a third opportunity beckons. Will we seize it, to take the best from each and shun their worst errors? Vienna built its system of peace on a balance of power sustained through the Concert of Europe by the leadership of Great Powers against a hegemony by any one of them. That was its merit. The mistake it made came from the internal structure of most of those Powers. For this required that they repress the two basic impulses of the modern age, nationalism and liberalism – the longing of men to be with their own kin under the same flag and free from a domestic absolutism, a foreign yoke, or both. In the peace-making of 1919, however, nationalism and liberal democracy enjoyed pride of place. That settlement failed and it did so because the concert of Great Powers broke down, which, in the hour of victory, had gathered to itself the balance of power. Leadership as it dissolved was at a discount – with the League of Nations as a system of security undergoing a consequent paralysis. And when the victors turned their backs on each other, the vanquished could again tear loose.

Twenty years after Versailles, humanity was convulsed once more. Why, then, did the peace of Vienna, despite its suppression of popular impulses, last a century? Why, at any rate, did Europe's local wars which followed Vienna not grow into continental or general wars? So long as no other Power could match Britain's world-wide sea power (and that exempted the Crimean War), a general war was ruled out. But why did none attempt to challenge seriously the European order on which her world status revolved? Why, as the Vienna settlement crumbled, were there no continental wars for a century? The answer may be this: that for fifty years after Vienna a greater, unified Germany had not yet been fashioned out of the various Germanic States. For what finally unbalanced Europe's distribution of power was the impact of a greater, expansionist Germany striving ruthlessly and inexorably towards an overweening hegemony. And when the era of Versailles allowed this greater Germany to hang on to territorial, strategic, and industrial resources out of which are forged the tools of domination it wrote its own obituary. The disintegration of the Austro-Hungarian Empire, the absence of Russia, the further decay of Turkey, presented Europe with changes of the utmost gravity. But chief among the differences which had intervened on the continent to distinguish the problem of Versailles from the problem of Vienna was the advent of a greater, unified Germany. And when the victors neglected subsequently to maintain their own balance of power against that cruel, tempestuous giant, they left themselves abjectly at his mercy. For beside the supernationalism of Germany, the national liberties of Europe cannot dwell unmolested. One or the other must go.

It would no doubt have been premature for Moscow and Teheran to confront this, the main key to world chaos before and after Versailles, in more specific terms. But on every issue they faced, their sense of direction was sound. While the solutions of 1919, and still more those of 1815, belong to their own day and age, there is much in their experience from which we might profit. The Vienna technique of leadership by Great Powers can be fused now with the Versailles programme of an international organization between equals for security. To reinsure it, a balance of power on a modified 1815 model, preponderating against any new bid for arbitrary domination, will protect the 1919 principle of national freedom and liberal democracy. The settlement of Vienna, while conscious of the realities of power, stultified itself when it repudiated the idea of progress. The era of Versailles, while imbued with ideas of progress, hastened its own demise when it later ignored the realities of power. For only through peace by power can victory be preserved and power itself thus be put to a creative use.

PART TWO

A Global Balance Takes Over

3 Risk and Paradox*

A global balance emerged when the cold war began and both sides, as they planned for the doom-laden impact of long-distance nuclear warfare, armed against each other so ominously. 'We may be likened to two scorpions in a bottle,' had been a description of the nuclear arms race by Dr J. Robert Oppenheimer, 'each capable of killing the other, but only at the risk of his own life.' Nobody knows how he would have described such a bottle with those lesser scorpions that, in addition to Britain, France and China, threaten to become so numerous in the last quarter of the twentieth century.

Immobilising the risks of the global contest before that, however, have been the paradoxes to which it also conduced. What these were and the interplay between them was suggested below during the mid-1950s.

'My Cousin Charles and I are perfectly agreed,' said King Francis I during his campaigns against the Emperor Charles V. 'We both want Milan.' Today, not only the prizes of war have changed but the way in which these can be won. A new consensus between rival camps, that the spoils of war would be consumed by war itself, is the supreme paradox of the cold war. In a conflict between East and West, even the nominal victors might be seared and scourged beyond repair. And, if war devours its own chief prizes, for what will an

*This essay was first published as an article, 'Paradoxes of the Cold War', in the *New Leader* (New York, 24 Jan 1955).

Various features of the new global balance were analysed by the present writer in *Reprieve From War* (The Macmillan Company, New York, 1950) pp. 7-12, 38-9, 50-9, 80-6, 111-19.

Also Lionel Gelber, *America in Britain's Place* (Frederick A. Praeger Inc, New York, 1961; Allen and Unwin, London, 1961) pp. 69-71.

The Oppenheimer quotation is from *Foreign Affairs* (New York, Jul 1953) p. 529.

aggressor fight? Is modern man technologically hoist by his own petard? Has he tapped the energies of nature only to defeat himself?

Until recently, the rise and fall of civilizations was regional rather than global in scope. In the Mediterranean basin, as one civilization waned, another waxed; Europe grew and expanded overseas; India and China have had rich legacies of their own to cultivate. Although many things both concrete and intangible might decline, be lost or demolished over the centuries, there has been a certain continuity in imponderables. The interplay of cultures runs through the story of the West. When these overlapped in time, there was something to hand down, there was history.

Today, it is this thread of civilization which may be cut. Hitherto, when any one society was jeopardized, space and time were ramparts behind which others elsewhere could proceed. Infernal devices, with their range, their speed and their desolating effect, can now destroy this saving continuity. A radioactive atmosphere, moreover, would spell the doom of the human race. But even if life could go on where the soil was unpolluted and where the backward, unenmeshed in industrialism, could fend for themselves, history will have been vain if the great past in which Orient and Occident share were to be wiped out. What preserves this continuity is the fact that the bell, if it tolls now, would toll for all. Cosmic hazards furnish cosmic deterrents.

Between war and peace, however, there may be a compromise, which, as in Trotsky's wry venture at Brest-Litovsk, is neither. A decivilizing capacity overtakes a civilizing one and, by its sheer extent, condemns the whole of mankind to perpetual crisis. In the twentieth century, the revolution of bigness has transformed American democracy; and, where political traditions have not been free, its mass techniques have organized the totalitarian state. By the same token, some gulfs may be bridged when the scale of world integration is enlarged; others may be widened. Europe, long the principal arena of international affairs, is now but the main sector of a global equilibrium in which two non-European colossi, a Eurasian and a North American, preside over vast counteracting systems of power. The risk of world war, however, is diminished by the prospect of furies which span the earth. The East, superior in land-air power, able to shuttle back and forth within interior territorial lines, can bog down if it overreaches itself. The West, having to stretch around the Sino-Soviet perimeter, compensates through emphasis on sea-air power, through a supporting ring of transoceanic alliances and scattered dependencies, through a comparative mobility. By themselves, the cities of Western Europe could be considered open to surprise air attack. But, if their Sino-Soviet counterparts are to be protected from reprisals as devastating, all other peripheral centres of Atlantic retribution would have to be expunged in the same faultlessly co-ordinated stroke.

Soviet air defenses might be better than ours and yet not be so impregnable as to offset the access to key areas provided by the West's forward bases. Encircled by the Axis in the Thirties, the Soviet Union has now brought upon itself another kind of encirclement. Some of the West's dispersed bases could be swept away by military conquest in Asia, by ideological subversion in Europe and Africa. But, even if they were, the further the East operates from its own domains the less effective it itself is equipped to be.

The paradox of Western Europe's vulnerability is that it no longer invites a total assault. Either of the giant adversaries could erase it from the map. But what Communist Russia desires is to control Western Europe, not to lay it waste. There again, bigness in war threatens to backfire. The Soviet Union might try to undermine Western Europe from within, to subdue it intact. As a going concern, it is the top prize of East-West contention. As an uninhabitable ruin, its peace could be no more than – to echo a classic phrase – the peace of the wilderness.

The global contest, that seesaw of pressure and counter-pressure, is militant, then, even where it is non-military. Ideology has been put to work by totalitarian regimes as an instrument of power. The Soviet's mass appeal across frontiers is not so restrictive. Nazism, with Teutonic self-idolatry, despised the weak; by crushing them at home but seeking them out abroad, Communism adds to Russian and Chinese strength. The East-West drama unfolds, moreover, when new elements have emerged on the world stage, demanding a voice. The East courts the oppressed of other lands and the disinherited of every race; the West parries its thrusts by grants of independence and measures to raise living standards.

But coexistence does not merely imply a curb on the impact of power. It means that in the most uncompromising of doctrines there must still be room for compromise. If hostile creeds were as absolute in practice as they are in theory, the relative peace of the cold war would be inconceivable. But ever since the wars of religion antagonistic systems have had to learn how to tolerate each other, how ideology and power must come to terms if national interest so requires. The East itself has, after all, been linked with the Nazis against the West and with the West against the Nazis; in the West's own array are some who can scarcely be deemed paragons of democratic virtue.

Survival in the cold war entails yet another paradox. Lest there be mutual extinction, a settling-down without formal settlement, a global armistice in which local violations are never allowed to get out of hand, has had to precede, rather than follow, large-scale warfare.

Is there any escape from the perils of so precarious a peace? Despite the global dimensions of the cold war, neutrals think that there might be. The question is still: Neutral against whom? The position of traditional neutrals (Sweden, Switzerland) is pretty much what it always has been. But, within the Western coalition itself, Communist parties are not the only source of neutralist sentiment. In free Europe, it springs from fear of annihilation, in free Asia from a denial of any nearby menace. Among Asian neutrals, the entire cause of the West is misrepresented – the aims to which it would devote its power as well as the manner in which that power is exercised. India ranks first in free Asia, and she is isolationist. Perhaps she assumes that she will be left by such a course to deepen her unity and improve her economy unmolested; perhaps her view of the East-West rift is a rationalization in the light of domestic needs. But when she is outspoken about the West and circumspect about the East, this differential treatment gives the show away. For she dare not admit that which must haunt her most and, with shadows looming from the north, still refuse to take sides. Another paradox ensues. Many European neutrals have no illusions about the ideological phase of the cold war; neutralism in Asia is governed by one.

Neutralism is a policy which a country chooses for itself. Neutralization is a status which others choose for it. And the latter might be an expedient which both East and West can accept at outlying disputed points. But neutralization has never been feasible in a sector as decisive for global preponderance as the two halves of post-Nazi Germany. Their reunion under a pact of neutralization must presuppose that each segment, the East's and the West's, will be relinquished by its patron. Will Moscow *reculer pour mieux sauter,* abandon them momentarily in order to embrace them both eventually? The answer is evident. If the Soviet Union could be trusted to forfeit its designs on the German makeweight other crucial accords might also be honoured and the cold war would cease. The wheel of Fortune must spin again before that is likely to occur. Meanwhile, when Germans are on their own, the East, with irredentist lands, brethren and trade to offer can outbid the West. There have been circumstances in which a pact of renunciation bred confidence. When signatories have no confidence in each other, it may make matters worse.

And that, too, is why armaments, atomic-hydrogen and conventional, have not been regulated. For these issues, while momentous, are secondary; prime counters in the East-West game, they are not the game itself. Nevertheless, they have magnified its dangers to an infinite degree. Tension might therefore slacken wherever specific piecemeal arrangements can be achieved – over the arms ratios, over Germany, over other European or Asian problems. But negotiations that are not one-sided, guarantees which endure, must reflect a stabilizing equipoise of force. Among signatories who lack faith in each other, treaties will have scant value unless they are underwritten by those sanctions of power through which competitively global stalemate is maintained.

Such safeguards offer a reprieve from war; to avert submission, we must still rely on peace by power. It is the irony of bigness that its universalizing techniques not only serve war better than peace; they permit totalitarian regimes to tighten their clutches. What must be avoided are remedies worse than the disease. There are no cure-alls, only palliatives which should keep the patient alive until the outlook for civilization is more promising.

Ground for hope remains. War has always been a gamble, but it is the ultimate paradox of the cold war that the odds beforehand against all-out aggression have never been so plain. The physical structure of the West might be less expendable, more exposed than that of the East; it is the genius of democracies that, short of utter cataclysm, they will rally and resume where they can. Dictatorships which seize the helm in one kind of chaos may perish in another; once their grip is loosened, an order breaks up which the captive and the enslaved will not rush to restore. Even that sword of ideology which is brandished by the East with such bravado may thus be turned against it; only free societies contain within the seeds of self-renewal. Dictatorships might muster strength for the moment. For democracies, the power to outlast them is the power that must tell in the end.

4 The New American Realism*

Under the old classic American isolationism, it was only within the Western Hemisphere that the United States, having expanded territorially nearer home, intervened abroad. Since Pearl Harbour her peacetime involvements (apart from wars in Korea and Vietnam) have been, if only through a far-flung series of treaties, without precedent for her.

'I accept the Universe!', exclaimed Margaret Fuller, an American transcendentalist, and 'By God, she'd better!' was the answering riposte from Thomas Carlyle. But, as far as the modern world is concerned, these two had left no room for progress or improvement. With the latter, it seemed after World War II, a realistic American leadership of the West must be correlated.

As far as the eighteenth century could discern the nature of a moral order in public affairs, the United States was, by her fundamental documents, dedicated to one. But that their free order at home relied upon a free order abroad, the Founding Fathers realized better than many of their twentieth century descendants. They understood the role of power; dividing it constitutionally, they could not let it go against the nation internationally. They had cut themselves off from George III; Jefferson and Madison perceived nevertheless that the maritime power of Britain and the territorial safety of the United States were indissolubly bound up together. Only through British command of the seas could the Monroe Doctrine itself command respect. Yet as nineteenth century Americans reforged their union in blood, and proceeded to build unmolested on this continent their free society, their own dependence on a free world order was lost from sight.

*A longer version of this essay was published as an article, 'America and World Order', in *Christianity and Crisis* (New York, 8 Dec 1952).

From Napoleon I to the Kaiser Wilhelm II the British were so successful in keeping open the sea lanes that world order could be taken for granted. Americans immersed themselves in their own contests of power; they forgot the primacy of power in world politics because, for formative years, they were too effortlessly the complacent beneficiaries of benevolent oceanic power.

During the American Civil War the North and British naval vessels barely averted a clash at sea.

They never grew accustomed to doing their share. Conscious of their own moral heritage, they waxed indignant at the immoral policies of European countries but admitted no connection between moral order and any world responsibility of their own.

As the twentieth century dawned the Anglo-American aspect of American world security was, however, plain to John Hay. And Theodore Roosevelt sensed it when, so as to ensure a Russo-Japanese equilibrium in the Pacific, he blazed a double trail by intervening in the gravest European crisis before 1914. Among American statesmen these were the first moderns.

In hemisphere relations their realism was the sort Americans condemned in others. In global affairs it was the sort the United States should have embraced but would not.

Even after World War I she still spurned it. From errors in statecraft Woodrow Wilson was not exempt. But he may be credited with going one step further when he pioneered permanent American guarantees – to France and to the League of Nations – so that a favourable system could be maintained. His endeavour to convert American ideals of moral order into a broader concept of world order invited the derision of Clemenceau and the scepticism of Lloyd George. They and their countries were, nevertheless, willing to give the plan a try; it was Americans themselves who would not back up ideas rooted as deeply in the nation's past as the isolationist escapism to which they reverted. The world of George Washington had vanished, but when the United States reneged on Wilsonian commitments she proposed to pick up where he left off.

Politically, she had contracted out of world order. Psychologically, her contribution to disorder was as profound. Hardly scratched by war, she had let down partners who were maimed physically and spiritually. There was scarcely a mistake made by them between 1919 and 1939 which they did not attribute to the fact that without the help of their richest associate they had no choice. Americans still lectured them on the higher moralities; the great moralizer became, by her abstention, the great demoralizer. And the United States demoralized not only through her negative behaviour; positive American influences were not good either. When Britain ruined herself by letting a strong Germanic power be revived she received much encouragement from across the Atlantic. Neutrality legislation by Congress may have been the outcome of the attacks on bankers and munition-makers then current. This, however, was but one phase of a wider campaign. In England John Maynard Keynes had warned against the economic consequences of the peace; quite as devastating were to be the intellectual consequences of Mr Keynes himself. Spurred on by him, American professors, authors and editors busily joined a sedulous Teutonic campaign to revise the history of the 1914 war so as to show that, in its origins, the poor Germans were more sinned against than sinning. As if to justify its rejection by the United States, the moral validity of the 1919 peace settlement was thereby not only undermined. The pre-Nazi aim of German nationalists, to reverse the victory of 1918, would thus be fostered by the victors' own self-demoralization. For when publicists and public men rate the moral claims of an antagonist above, or equal to, those of our free world order there can be little moral conviction in our cause.

To change one's mind is a democratic privilege. But leadership, having a test to pass, is something else again. Ground for confidence must, in a complex society with a moral legacy, be either practical, moral or both; but when it is neither the one nor the other, there is no such ground. After the atomic spy trials in Canada, the United States and Britain, the hazards of pro-Soviet betrayal from within should not be underestimated. But, by the same token, how wholesome can the atmosphere be when mentors of freedom – political and diplomatic, journalistic and academic – are many of those who so recently were among the most insistent of demoralizers; men who, whether on the Right or the Left, did more to immobilize our free world order than could any wretched Communist prior to the ghastly traffic in atomic plans and research?* After 1919 it was playing the enemy's game to keep attention focused on the peace treaties – those which proved unenforceable being modified in practice anyway. The impact of the warmakers rather than the designs of the peacemakers was what had impaired the economy of Europe. Britain and France lost their grip after 1918; the United States would neither support nor supplant them. Together all three were preponderant in 1919. By 1939 they had themselves sapped the foundations of power on which alone their free world order could rest.

Against the same German militarism we won again in 1945. But the further debility of Western Europe is what permits Russian expansion to be resumed; is what has set upon the shoulders of the United States a burden which is so disproportionate because it is so late. The menace of renewed disorder nowadays stems from the disorder which the free peoples themselves facilitated in the twenties and thirties. Reinhold Niebuhr devoted a volume to the irony of American history. But the supreme irony occurs when misconceptions of history form the stuff of history.

Charter implementation in Korea, the rearmament of the West, an Atlantic unity which stretches out to the Eastern Mediterranean – such are, at last, the concrete underpinnings of a free world order. In conquered Germany – perhaps also in Japan – the West may once more undo with one hand what it has done with the other. But, generally speaking, the United States has been undergoing a revolution in attitude. And this in turn had to be impelled by a revolution in ideas. There may be isolationist backslidings; American internationalism is, on the whole, here to stay. The position of the United States cannot alter, however, without a change in

*The present writer explored these questions in *The American Anarchy (Democracy in an Era of Bigness)* (Henry Schuman, Inc, New York, 1953) pp. 88-139. That book used the concept of 'organisational man' some years before it was adapted to the requirements of a best-seller.

outlook upon major components of world affairs. Nationalism, ideology and power are no longer phenomena to be contemplated from the distance but elements to be pondered in the framing of policy.

The result is a new American realism. Between the wars the high-minded were lukewarm about the defense of the West because the power substratum of our free world order was not all that it should be. In the Occident they felt or were grieved by economic injustice; in the Orient they hated colonialism and the exploitation of colored races by white. Blinded by our own transgressions, perfectionists thereby smoothed a path for aggressors whose iniquities were so much worse. And nowadays, too, the Moscow line may be taken up where, as in Europe and Asia, economic conditions are propitious; but in the United States it is only among the most unreconstructed demoralizers that prewar illusions have not been dispelled. Rational Americans do not renounce their own democracy because of the moral ambiguities which reside within it. So also they are learning to accept much in our free world order that is ambivalent. The harm done to civilized values by utopian revolutionaries has, furthermore, shed cruel light on misdirected idealism. If we cherish these, we must preserve that world order in which alone they may yet have a better chance.

Even a force like nationalism will seem to Americans good or bad according to circumstances. Federal schemes, as urged by the United States, would curb it in Western Europe; in Asia it is now a torch of liberation, now one of chauvinism, often both simultaneously. In Western Europe the disorder it generates has been immeasurably destructive; among European nations subjugated by the Soviet Union it may emerge as a weapon of freedom. Washington would thus have nationalism soft-pedalled in one quarter, stimulated in another.

There is, however, nothing irreconcilable between the defensive needs of the West and the legitimate demands of each particular nationalist ideology in non-Soviet Asia. Under Communist rule the latter assuredly would not be fulfilled. But so far as the West itself, with its concept of a free world order, sponsors an ideology which is a universal one, it must withstand the universalist ideology of the Soviet credo. For Moscow also has a concept of world order; that is why the drive to universalize Communist ideology is so relentless. And it is the use made of nationalism which in fact illustrates how the two rival world ideologies, that of the East and that of the West, differ from each other. In Soviet calculations Communist universalism has become an instrument of Russia's own national power; the West, contrariwise, hopes to employ national power so as to extend more universally the benefits of a free world order, so that its own nationalism may be robbed of its sting. To spread social justice is morally right in itself; strategically it can do a lot towards staving off the onrush of the Communist evangel. Yet it is also significant that from Peking to Prague Communist ideas have only triumphed where Russian armed power was either on the spot or hovered nearby. From Prague to Peking they can only be combatted under a counteracting wing of stabilizing power.

Such is the new realism. In global affairs it took two catastrophic wars to teach the United States that a free world order, lest it be overpowered, must exert power. That power corrupts we know. Yet, without power, liberty itself may be crushed. Power devoid of moral controls is the sheerest expediency; law alone, as the wars of the century demonstrate, is impotent. Power behind the law may uphold an order of power which is at once ethical and viable. Realism, so uncongenial to the idealistic mentality, has always been identified with the unmoral. A blend of the two is the aim of the new realism. Machiavelli will sit at the council table. But others also should have as big a voice.

5 The Problem of German Reunification Before *Ostpolitik**

Unity is no longer a problem for Germans themselves to decide. Why this is so not all of them grasp even now. But they could accept the inevitable with less reluctance after Konrad Adenauer put the Bonn Republic on its feet. And new, broader international trends would have to change once more before the two Germanies might come together again.

That this will not soon occur was the premise of Ostpolitik *as conceived by Herr Willy Brandt. But the position had been sufficiently complicated before he took office. By 1960, when this essay was first published, nothing had done more than East-West friction over the two Germanies to aggravate the European phase of the global contest.*

Few are the concepts upon which democracies and dictatorships may vent a common spleen. The *status quo* has, nevertheless, been among them. Wider freedoms were said to be impeded when, after World War I, the liberal-minded began to denounce it; against Communist and Nazi threats alike it functioned, all the same, as a prop of a free world order. And now once more, in the East-West dispute over German reunification, the same paradox recurs. Even those with a stake in the *status quo* are loath to admit it.

The French, for example, bury outworn enmities when they second the idea of reunion between the two Germanys. Yet all projects for that semi-continental unity of which Franco-German partnership is the core must take a divided Germany as their premise.

In their European policies, moreover, English-speaking allies have also been ambiguous. Proposing that the German *status quo* be altered, the United States and Britain have likewise had a paramount interest in its preservation. To re-

*This essay was first published as an article, 'East, West and the German Status Quo', in *Christianity and Crisis* (New York, 22 Feb 1960).

store the major segment of German power was to reanimate German national impulses. Washington and London hoped that these might be harnessed for the defense of the West. But it is only under circumstances inimical to the West that they can finally be fulfilled. Washington assumed that Russia would somehow relinquish her grip on East Germany; Moscow's prerequisite for the reunion of the two Germanys has, nevertheless, always been the detachment of the Bonn Republic from the West. For Germany is to Western Europe what Western Europe is to the global balance – a makeweight that can, geographically and technologically, turn the scales.

And this is why a reunified Germany that may belong to the West was, despite all that Western statesmen said and did, never in the cards. Moscow's bargaining advantage has been clear from the outset. The West, having established and released it, ceded to the Bonn Republic the freedom to choose between East and West. But Russia grants her German vassal no such option. She can thereby forbid German reunification on Western terms. It must either be done as she wishes or not at all. The existing equilibrium is for English-speaking allies, as well as for France, the one viable alternative.

A divided Germany was, it so happens, what the Big Three contemplated during World War II. They could scarcely foresee how it would be polarized between them in any post-war contest of their own. Decentralizing trends were reversed, at any rate, as soon as President Truman took office. And today it is the *status quo* from which West Germans themselves also benefit. The Bonn Republic had to be built up before it could ever expect to negotiate with the East from strength. It owes everything to the Anglo-American presence, and from a Western orientation there is still much to be gained.

Will a more irrational temper supervene? Would the Bonn Republic, prone to the frustrations of irredentism, yet leave its French partner and other Western allies in the lurch? After World War I the German Right strove to reverse the verdict of 1918 by dealing with Moscow; before the verdict of 1945 can be reversed, however, it is a Soviet veto that must now be removed. Chancellor Adenauer renounced a concept of national interest that runs from Tauroggen through the diplomacy of Bismarck to the Rapallo and Nazi-Soviet pact. But the reunification of the two Germanys has also been Bonn's objective and only with Moscow's assent can this be achieved.

The dilemma of the West will be evident and to it, alas, there is no watertight solution. It was a united Germany that, in recurrent German wars, demolished the European balance of power and destroyed ramparts against any counter-thrust from the East; it is access to a divided Germany that would enable the United States, Britain and Canada to combine with continental allies in shoring up a key sector of a global equilibrium. The Bonn Republic emerged under the sheltering wing of that equilibrium and, as long as they need it for their security, West Germans themselves must boggle over any one-sided modification of the German *status quo*. But if the time should ever come when they want reunification more than other things the defense of the West will suffer.

Unsettling, too, has been the impact of the arms race on the Bonn Republic. Can this be slackened without attenuating links between West Germany and the West? One point must be remembered when ingenious schemes for a more tolerable *modus vivendi* are broached: the arms race is a symptom of a deeper political malaise; only when the one is checked can the other be fully curtailed. The continental framework of counteracting power might be revamped. It will only be safe if an existing equilibrium is reproduced within it. To grant Soviet demands that NATO bases be dismantled would be for the West European sector of Western strategy to immobilize itself. And when the countervailing defenses of the West contract, Russian power, shorn of opposition, might again expand gratuitously.

The German *status quo* is far from ideal. Through it an existing equilibrium has been preserved. Some in the West are disposed to purchase reunification by neutralizing Germany; Moscow would now disarm and neutralize the two separated German sovereignties. But American, British and Canadian forces have NATO obligations to carry out; either proposal would handicap them in the performance of their duties.

A neutralization of Germany, as a whole or in part, entails the withdrawal of NATO and Soviet troops from German territory. But the Russian imperium gives ample space in which Soviet forces that have been pulled back from East

Germany can be wheeled about and sped westward again. Troops from extra-continental NATO allies would, however, have to be concentrated into the relatively narrow coastal fringe of France and the Low Countries; lacking room for deployment, they might be more exposed to assault, manned and missile, from the air.

NATO is the operational machinery of the North Atlantic Alliance and the strategic position was made no easier for France or the West when, as de Gaulle evicted its troops from her soil, the political side also departed. For all her Cartesian logic and splendid diction, France, as the first non-NATO member of the North Atlantic Alliance, never made clear why others should do more for her defense than she must do for others. Nor did she forgive the English-speaking peoples for liberating her from Petain and Hitler alike.

And what if forces thus jeopardized were evacuated from the European continent beforehand? Barriers to Russian domination, as the United States retires into Fortress America, will have fallen.

Nor is this all. Neutrality as the price of reunification might require East-West guarantees. Yet these cannot be enforced if oversea powers no longer have a tenable foothold on the European continent. The difficulty would not arise if the two Germanys were reunited on Western terms. But short of that, it is through the Bonn Republic that NATO front lines have been drawn. A reunited Germany may be the goal of Western statesmen, but it is upon a divided Germany that Western defense is predicated.

Meanwhile Russian interests are also served by the German *status quo*. Berlin has been an island of freedom in a Communist sea; and it will cease to be one when occupation troops from the United States, Britain and France depart. Ostensibly, their withdrawal would alter the German *status quo*; in fact, this must simplify its maintenance behind the Iron Curtain.

Moscow is, for the moment, unable to alter the *status quo* in West Germany; Communist rule in East Germany is consolidated instead. And that is why Russia has advocated a confederation of the two Germanys; one in which sundered halves may negotiate any further unity between themselves, but in which East Germany is also to retain its Communist character. No loose grouping can be approved which stipulates that the Bonn Republic must discard its ties with the West or in which an East German component acts as a Trojan Horse within the walls of the West. And what this means will be plain. The only safe measures are those which, by pressure and counter-pressure, reduplicate the German *status quo* in a new form.

Is the German *status quo* a peril to peace? The Berlin situation derives from it and as long as this lasts there might be trouble. But in another respect it may not be as unstable as many believe. In June 1953, when East Germany rebelled against the local Communist regime, the Bonn Republic had not yet been rearmed. But would regular or irregular troops from West Germany now go to the support of another insurrection and thus embroil the entire NATO alliance with the East? They might.

West Germans, however, are largely Catholic and liberal-conservative, East Germans Protestant and Socialist; for the liberation of East German kinsmen, West Germans have displayed no consuming ardor. Apprehensive over their own involvement in the nuclear-missile age, they do not seem bent on military adventure. Reunification may be negotiated one day – if not through the West, then with the East. West Germans are not likely to fight for it.

Then, too, the German *status quo* helps fortify Communist discipline. Nowadays East Germany is fairly docile. Apart from Berlin, it can act as an ideological buffer between provocative Western influences and the remainder of the Soviet imperium.

A divided Germany is, furthermore, what other captive nations desire their Russian overlord to maintain. As between two recent invaders, the German and the Russian, they still regard the Russians as the lesser evil; it is by fending off the apparition of another strong Germany that Moscow elicits from them a modicum of unenforced obedience, even consent. If Soviet forces were pulled back, Poland, for one, might obtain more autonomy. But her plan for East-West disengagement was also geared in with Moscow's project for a confederation of two disarmed, neutralized German states. Poles may pray for less constraint in a Russian sphere, but it is from the prospect of a German sphere that they recoil most.

And Warsaw's attitude is not unintelligible. During World War II, the Soviet Union redrew the boundaries of occupied German and Polish territory; their final demarcation, it was decided at Potsdam in 1945, would have to await a German peace treaty. Together with East Prussia, Russia filched a large slice of eastern Poland and compensated Poland with Pomerania and Silesia, former German provinces to which she clings fiercely.

In the surrender of these Oder-Neisse lands the Communist regime of East Germany has had to acquiesce. The Bonn Republic would, however, be less amenable. Its compliance may be withheld as a bargaining card when reunification is negotiated; but their reacquisition is a dream that refugees from lost German territories keep alive. Warsaw, at any rate, suspects that Bonn's real aim is the reunion of the two Germanys within prewar (1937) boundaries.

President de Gaulle recognized that there can be no retrocession of the Oder-Neisse lands and his candor annoyed West Germans. The upshot is that, in Polish eyes, the Russian sway over East Germany figures as a guarantee of Poland's own western frontier. Not that she is without anxiety on this score. What if Moscow offers the Oder-Neisse lands to the irredentists of Bonn as a bribe? It is at Poland's expense that a German reunification on Russian terms may be expedited.

Nor is it an imaginary bogey by which she is frightened. From Frederick the Great to the Nazi-Soviet Pact, the partition of Poland has always been the outcome of Russo-German agreements. The sight of a divided Germany is what now reconciles Poles to their own harsh fate. In the Soviet imperium, moreover, Poland is not the only one who speaks from tragic experience. Czechoslovakia is afraid that Sudeten areas might, as at Munich, again be stolen by a greater Germany. If the two Germanys were reunified on Russian terms, a staggering blow would be inflicted globally on the West. Yet locally, too, this must be anathema to Soviet captive states.

And this is another reason why the Western powers may be served best by the existing equilibrium. The British and French were to join the United States in sponsoring the idea of reunification. But none of them can neglect the cause of others who languish under a Soviet yoke. They have welcomed the fact that Poland is neither as oppressed nor as oppressive as she was; nothing could as swiftly drive her back into Moscow's protective embrace as the rebirth of a greater Germany. Captive peoples lose heart whenever East and West vie for the *beaux yeux* of the Bonn Republic. For their ordeal the West often expresses sympathy. Yet solicitude and efforts at reunification have implicitly been at odds.

It is, moreover, not only East Europeans who have been haunted by the spectre of another Russo-German accord. Dread of a second Nazi-Soviet Pact before victory was clinched may have been the clue to Yalta in 1945. No Russo-German alliance will materialize as long as the Bonn Republic stays aligned with the West; in that alignment, nevertheless, the German *status quo* is presupposed. For it is a crowning irony that the West must strive to change an equilibrium which, from the Western standpoint, is best left unchanged.

6 Peaceful Coexistence or a Durable Peace?*

How peace may be prolonged between major rival camps was explored in this essay during the summer of 1964 from two points of view. The first was the kind of detente that might or might not be feasible in a global contest. The second was how well the United Nations might do.

The West has not always presented a common front over policies of detente with Russia or China. By the same token some have done better in the world body than others. But even a mixed bag is better than none.

Peaceful coexistence, as Moscow expounds it, is a formula for political warfare without war, a slogan for peace that is also a battle-cry. A proposition that suits Soviet purposes, it has not been accepted in the West – yet only by mutual consent can the Cold War be concluded. The Soviet theory of peaceful coexistence is, from the standpoint of the West, a contradiction in terms. But time may provide us with a solution: the Soviet Union needs peace as much as any nation. The conditions of peace will be decided by that fundamental fact, not by the Kremlin's attempts to prescribe them unilaterally in advance.

What the Kremlin wants is clear. It would now like to attain the aims of Marx and Lenin by the methods of Gandhi. Yet non-violence, in a game being played for keeps, is not enough. In the vein of the Kellogg-Briand Pact and the United Nations Charter, Chairman Khrushchev proposed the outlawry of war over most territorial disputes. But freedom is threatened so long as one party has hegemonic ambitions, and while freedom remains in danger there can be no durable peace. Even a limited *détente* could furnish a reprieve from

*This essay was first published as an article in *Orbis* (Philadelphia, Summer 1964). Paragraphs that are now irrelevant have been deleted.

war. There can, however, be no durable peace until the Soviet system is geared for one.

The hopes of mankind for peace, or at least a reduction of tensions, have been dashed more than once, Nevertheless, the Soviet Union and the West lean periodically toward some *modus vivendi* because circumstances without precedent compel them to do so. Latter-day peacemaking will bear scant resemblance to what was done at Vienna in 1815 or at Paris in 1919. The Cold War has not been fought like traditional wars, and the modalities of settlement may be just as untraditional. In the global nuclear-missile age an armistice must *precede* large-scale hostilities and, as between the USSR and the West, there can be neither victors nor vanquished after negotiations are concluded.

Victory, even though deferred, remains the Soviet objective. Soviet leaders make no secret of this; it is the professed purpose of their peaceful coexistence strategy. Specific issues on the East-West agenda are not, then, the only stumbling-blocks; a limited *détente* is the most we can hope for until there is a change of heart in Moscow. Yet a limited *détente* will be better than none. The circumstances that have predisposed the Soviets toward a limited *détente* might in the interim acquire a momentum of their own. Like her adversaries in the West, the Soviet Union has shunned war lest it get out of control. But peace may get out of control if all does not go according to the Kremlin's plan. The very exigencies that have called forth a strategy of peaceful coexistence might reshape it.

Captive states are not the most enthusiastic of allies. The East European satellites, nevertheless, depend on Moscow to keep the Germanys divided and thus stave off the specter of another greater German Reich – while, for an inner counterpoise against Moscow, some also look to Peking. As dissension with Communist China perturbs the Soviet Union, its leaders, ironically, may discover that the West might yet be a less implacable foe than their own major ally.

Not that it is unusual for allies to fall out. If there has been surprise on this occasion, it may be due to an overrating of the ideological bond between Moscow and Peking. As an adjunct of power, such a bond is highly useful when employed against common foes. Yet doctrinal affinities, as Yugoslavia's early postwar quarrel with the Soviet Union revealed, do not stand alone. East Germans would scarcely have rebelled in 1953, nor would Poles and Hungarians have done the same in 1956, if less drastic forms of divergence from a Soviet overlord had been available.

The same applied to the tragic Czechoslovak bid for more independence in 1968.

But some communist states can follow their own bent. And when they do, it is the national interest, with them as with the Soviet Union herself, that comes first. Ideology, as a concomitant, may be utilized abroad as far as expedient. When power is the primary element, it is considerations of power that must ultimately prevail.

For a while, to be sure, considerations of power together with doctrinal affinities did provide the Soviet Union and Communist China with common interests. Not since the turn of the century had there been so little to distract the Soviet Union on her East Asian frontiers. This situation emboldened her after World War II to promote with impunity the communist cause elsewhere.

But now peaceful coexistence, as a more subtle program for communist hegemony in the nuclear-missle age, may be too crude for the West and not sufficiently crude for the Kremlin's own jealous Chinese disciples. Perhaps when the Communist Chinese originally deemed war with capitalist countries inevitable it was more the spirit of Machiavelli than of Marx and Lenin that incited them – the most sinister of expectations that, if the Soviet Union bore the brunt, Communist China would come out on top. Today, however, when all peoples might be consumed by global war, we seem to hear less of such cosmic levity. Instead, Communist China accepts recognition from Gaullist France and attempts to win Africans and Asians to her side. Her campaign against the Soviet Union and the West has not been toned down. Nobody knows how far a nation that is the greatest of 'have-nots' will carry old territorial grievances against its much larger northern neighbor. But we can be certain that distraction in the Orient will inhibit the Soviets' freedom of maneuver everywhere else.

This may be one of those quandaries that grow the more perplexing the more one seeks to escape them. Chinese ill-will prevents the Soviet Union from acting with aplomb against the West; yet, if the Soviets act with the West, Communist China might gain the loyalty of communist parties elsewhere and the leadership of the East. Behind the facade of an intramural feud over ideology there is thus a Sino-Soviet dispute over power, over Moscow's own status in the Sino-Soviet imperium, and thus over Moscow's place in the world. For the moment, if this dispute accentuates factional quarrels within the walls of the Kremlin, the Soviet Union may vacillate between Peking and the West, wavering between reconciliation with the West today and defiance of the West tomorrow, switching the Cold War off and on. It is Moscow's own narrowing range of choice which might, nevertheless, distinguish new Soviet peace offensives from old ones.

Foreign affairs interact with domestic affairs: The Kremlin, seemingly caught in a strategic box, finds a related one on the home front just as confining. If Soviet agricultural production cannot be increased substantially, a greater proportion of industrial resources may have to be diverted from the manufacture of arms or even from experiments in space, and grain supplies may again have to be purchased from the West. Although the Soviets recently reported an improvement in domestic agriculture, there will also have to be supplies of another kind from the West if Soviet agricultural productivity is to be increased: the Soviet Union will need to import equipment to expand its agriculturally-related chemical industries. But the Soviet Union must have a lull on the foreign front before she can concentrate upon domestic problems. Until such time the West itself will remain divided over the extent to which some of the Cold War restrictions upon trade should be lifted.

Would the Soviet Union, after overcoming recent embarrassments and setbacks at home and abroad, be in a better position than ever to take advantage of the West? Uncertainty about the answer to that question will beset efforts toward a *détente*. However, the Soviet Union can revive her all-out Cold War policies only when the challenge of Communist China has waned; when captive states in Eastern Europe are more docile; and when the West has lowered its guard irrecoverably. Perhaps the Soviet people, having had a taste of the good life and wanting more rather than less, will make it difficult for any Soviet regime to backtrack.

It has been suggested that a *détente* with Communist China, rather than the Soviet Union, might be more advantageous for the West. But this is not a viable alternative. For one thing, if the Communist Chinese were more amenable, the Soviet Union itself could deal with Peking and thus would not have to seek a *détente* with the West. Then, too, an accommodation between the USSR and the West may, in Moscow's reckoning, provide security to the Soviets against a belligerent and aggressive Chinese neighbor. If the West were to build up Communist China against the Soviets, it would only heighten Moscow's fears of the West and of Peking. We would have removed one of the Soviet Union's reasons for a *détente* with the United States. We would still live in a world in which the two nuclear giants stood armed against one another, while China and France had also acquired nuclear weapons. It is, above all, an accommodation between two colossi, the Soviet Union and the United States, that is of crucial importance.

Detente with both Russia and China simultaneously became the goal of Presidents Nixon and Ford as well as Secretary Kissinger. Some of America's European allies had long pursued similar policies but these could not be as decisive.

It should be added that the three lesser nuclear Powers (India only being poised so far on the brink) vary greatly in their strategy. As long as there is so much animosity between China and Russia, it is more against the Soviet Union than the West that China pursues nuclear preparedness.

Like some latter-day Ishmaelite, though, Gaullist France did, at one juncture, plan her preparedness (in the spirit of Louis XIV and Vauban) à tous azimuts – *at all points of the compass. About this she is less irrational now. Despite baneful eccentricities, the French have ceased at least also to set sights on their own Atlantic allies.*

The roles of power and ideology should be reassessed if it is the interplay between them that will determine the prospects for peace. Nor are they the only factors which will be affected by a *détente*. Its effect upon neutralists and the United Nations must also be considered.

Power cannot be eliminated. There may be a proportionate decline in arms establishments, but power to enforce agreements between rival camps and to handle third parties will have to be retained. World War II could have been avoided if, after World War I, the West had recognized power realities. In a negative sense that conflict vindicated a school of thought which had insisted upon peace through power as the surest way of protecting civilized society from surrender or war: this school of thought would be vindicated positively if the West, by arraying its power against the East, could induce the Soviets to take a more conciliatory course. The West now perceives that there is nothing automatic about a free world order. It has to be supported without surcease.

This would seem to be the lesson impressed upon Moscow by that most momentous of duels, the encounter between Kennedy and Khrushchev over Soviet missiles in Cuba. But such a lesson has not been fully learned as yet. For after the Cuban showdown there was renewed emphasis upon ideological competition, a less devastating form of East-West strife. 'Containment' and 'positions of strength' were the verbalizations of an earlier concept of peace by power adapted to the postwar era; if that approach had not succeeded so well, Moscow and Peking would not denounce it with such venom. This concept remains valid. The Kremlin deludes itself if it imagines that it has, in ideological competition, a safe alternative through which it can loosen the grip of the West.

Peaceful coexistence will give ideological competition its chance, although its Soviet version sounds less than peaceful. Where national liberation movements are directed against the West rather than the communists, Peking backs them up; and in that sphere, too, Moscow may not allow the Chinese communists to reap all the benefits. Therefore the Soviets still bless, if only by rote, the revolutionary struggle of 'subject peoples' against 'foreign oppressors' and of 'workers' against 'exploiters.'

Other inconsistencies are more far-reaching. Soviet communism may either coexist amicably with a rival system or conspire against it: the West cannot assent when there is an endeavor to do both. Peaceful coexistence assumes that the Soviet Union can live in the short run with the democracies of the West while attempting to communize them; it also assumes that the ideological and power elements in the East-West contest can be separated from each other. Neither assumption is correct.

Neutralists and the United Nations have, besides, exerted some influence upon the Cold War, but its impact has been greater upon them. With the origins of a *détente* they would, similarly, have little to do. Yet, such a development could scarcely leave them indifferent.

Not all the emergent peoples have shunned Cold War alignments. But all, aligned and unaligned, who dwell beyond the frontiers of the Sino-Soviet imperium have had their independence underwritten by the power of the West. Most of them could have done very little to help maintain this power; the influence they exercized did not derive from the size of the contribution they could make but from the trouble they could stir up. For it was during the Cold War that Western overseas empires, badly shaken by World War II, received their *coup de grâce.* The Soviet Union, with or without Communist China, would have become the main patron of former dependencies if independence had been withheld. Here, then, is another contemporary paradox: Most of the emergent peoples lack power, yet the global power balance would have been upset if the communists could have taken them over.

Neutralism was the best policy for many of the emergent peoples. This presupposed that they would remain above the ideological battle. But this they did not all do. Some neutralists railed more at the West than at the East. And they could get away with such 'unneutral' behavior as long as the titans courted them.

Even when the USSR vies with the West in offering economic aid to emergent peoples, she may have a burgeoning community of interest with it – one with which political warfare against the West would interfere. Although such a community of interest does not yet exist, industrialized nations do realise that they must attempt to prevent any further widening of the gap between themselves and developing countries. The industrial West as well as the Soviet Union will hardly relish the role of 'milch cow' to the new states. The Soviet Union, although it may be overextended in a number of spheres, is suffering growing-pains rather than arrested growth. And overextension is a burden that a *détente* with the West would lighten.

In their penetration of more-distant lands, Moscow and Peking have been trying not only to outdo the West but to compete with each other. Communist China, with fewer economic surpluses, is not as well equipped as the USSR or the West for such a venture. If, however, Peking mixes race with ideology, she might exert a magnetic attraction on some of the other 'have-nots.' Through a realignment of colored peoples against white, under the Chinese banner, Communist China might contrive to reassert herself. Such a contingency would bedevil the future for the Soviet Union as well as the West. Only in unison with the West can Moscow combat it. But here, again, it will be difficult for the Kremlin to co-operate with the West as long as it wages political warfare against the West.

The West has not been of one mind on the topic of emergent peoples. Not only have the weak, thanks to propitiation by East and West, acquired an unreal strength; at various junctures the solidarity of the West has also been impaired. So eager at times was the United States, with an eye on Moscow and Peking, to cosset neutralists that during the Suez and Congolese crises of the 1950s and 1960s she downgraded vital ties with major allies.

Neutralism had been anathema to John Foster Dulles when he served as Dwight Eisenhower's Secretary of State. A later chapter will suggest various hypotheses for a sudden about-face by Washington during the Anglo-French coercion of Egypt in 1956.

In Western Europe the upshot was a more detached attitude toward American leadership, as well as an accelerated drive toward the foundation of the Common Market. To this motive for European unity, American champions of an enlarged Community never paid heed. Nor did the United States find the very emergent peoples on whose behalf she has done so much any more responsive.

Then, too, a *rapprochement* between the West and the

Soviet Union might also affect the United Nations. In this international forum, as never before and as nowhere else, the poor and ineffectual could foregather, enhance their tactical strength and, as between East and West, bring it to bear. The United Nations was reduced to comparative impotence by the East-West feud; more recently it has been reduced to near-bankruptcy by a quarrel within the West, as well as between West and East, over its peace-keeping functions. Significant, too, is the fact that it has only been able to discharge these duties in territories – Sinai-Gaza, the Congo and Cyprus, but not Hungary and Tibet – to which the West rather than the East has enjoyed strategic access.

There is still a United Nations Emergency Force in Cyprus. One had been ejected from Sinai, however, by President Nasser of Egypt as he got ready in 1967 for yet another attack on Israel. In the October war of 1973 Egypt crossed the Suez Canal, and a United Nations Emergency Force again patrolled cease-fire lines in the Sinai Peninsula between Egypt and Israel. There was also a UN Disengagement Observer Force on the Golan Heights, the embattled front between Israel and Syria.

Peace-keeping is not a task that the United Nations will undertake lightly in the future. Nor were the interests of the West always served by its interventions as they might have been.

In the General Assembly, all the same, the impoverished and disinherited now hold the balance of voting power. Behind this facade, it is the West's own power for peace that has enabled the world organization to endure. The main transactions in global politics could not be funneled through the United Nations during the Cold War. There may be more recourse to it if the Cold War is settled.

The seating of Communist China could present a serious obstacle. Should this be arranged, the Security Council might be enlarged with nonpermanent seats allocated to other Afro-Asian members. But the Chinese seat would be a permanent one and would give Peking the prerogative of the veto. It was to spite the West that the Soviet Union cast many of her vetoes in the Security Council; it might be against both the Soviet Union and the West that Communist China would similarly make herself felt. Yet to attain influence in other UN organs, underdeveloped countries would have to back her. That she could not get by antagonizing them.

Peking's instrument of policy would be a counter-racism which white domination itself fanned in the Orient. Asian neighbors who may concur with this are the satellite and client states of Communist China as well as other anti-Western countries. As for African countries (which have a numerical preponderance in the Afro-Asian bloc and which the Chinese seem to be trying harder than the Soviets to penetrate), a militant counter-racism would also appeal to the less moderate among them. But for the member-states of the Afro-Asian bloc, the refusal of Communist China to sign the partial nuclear test ban must have seemed ominous. Nor has Peking, by its coercion of Tibet and aggression against India, endeared itself to most of free Asia. Communist China's assault on India may, in fact, have been as self-defeating as the Kremlin's missile gambit in Cuba proved to be. For that episode not only sharpened cleavages in the Sino-Soviet camp, it also brought the first faint signs of common interest among Russia, India and the West. Counter-racism, in other words, has not provided an answer to India's pressing economic and military problems. It may not provide an answer for those in the Orient who still take their cue from New Delhi.

If that is so, Communist China might, by her presence, have less of an impact on the United Nations than is anticipated. The Afro-Asian neutralists would have to line up behind her before their tactical strength could be converted into real strength – into the substance of power within the world organization and beyond it. This they might hesitate to do, fearing that they might fall into the clutches of Communist China or at best lose needed economic assistance from the 'white' nations. No such hazard lurks in a more modest neutral course. It would be better for the weak to take a place in the United Nations commensurate with their actual power, and better for the United Nations if the strong, with their greater responsibilities, did the same.

Developing countries would like nowadays to employ the export of raw materials as a lever for improving their status. But most of them started late in the game and it may not be as practicable for them, as for Arab oil States, to conserve or stockpile such natural products. Early sale abroad is essential when, among so many, starvation is, or may soon be, rife.

Their plight has been exacerbated by a rise in oil prices to which, it so happens, Arab oil States contributed lucratively – poor recompense for an Afro-Asian shift at the United Nations from a pro-Israel to a pro-Arab stance.

We should avoid the temptation to assign to the United Nations a role beyond its capacities. There are some in the West who, with perspicacity, deride the international organization. For their part, the communists have sought to subordinate its machinery to their global objectives. And so the United Nations must be saved from its friends as well as its foes.

Out of the present organization may come a Parliament of Man, but such a fulfilment is far off. A world body composed largely of regimes that cannot speak for their own people cannot speak adequately for mankind – or serve as its mentor. NATO, to be sure, also includes authoritarian regimes who nevertheless do help, by their commitment to the West, to uphold a free world order. The United Nations, on the other hand, while a beneficiary of what the West does, has been assigned a task that cuts across rival ideologies. Its membership roster must therefore be still more diverse: democracies that speak authentically for their own people; dictatorships, Left and Right, which may not; and latter-day versions of benevolent despotism that might be more democratic if only they could. This is peaceful coexistence as it ought to be. But the UN, with its mixture of political systems, cannot be regarded as democratically representative of the world's peoples. Thus, we should not put an undue value upon the 'conscience of mankind' as it speaks to us through various organs, for to do so is to debase the values of the Charter itself.

To understate the case for the world organization would be as wrong as to overstate it. A proper view of the United

Nations must rest on the fact that it has been on the outer edge rather than in the center of the East-West contest, and that therefore it should not be asked to regulate forces at whose mercy it still lies. For some missions it is the most appropriate of instruments; others could prove too onerous for it. If the UN is asked to undertake assignments beyond its capacity, more harm than good will have been done; peace itself might suffer. A dearth of funds is not all that frustrates the United Nations. It might rue the day on which it is granted more authority than it has earned, more than it can prudently bear.

There will still be much for the international organization to do. Though it falls short of the objectives set by its founders, the United Nations is no mere talking-shop. The work of the specialized agencies has been indispensable. Only an organization such as the UN could have policed accessible strategic trouble spots. Nowhere else can so many spokesmen for states, East and West, aligned and unaligned, large and small, of every race, color and creed, discuss mutual problems so conveniently – or meet at all. There may be less to hamper the United Nations externally, and less to distort it internally, if there is a *détente* between the Soviet Union and the West. Until there is one, the functions of that body cannot be broadened.

Meanwhile, the most deadly feature of the global contest is the arms race. No *détente* will be complete until this is slowed down. It may be too soon to establish an international police force on a permanent basis; it may be too late to prevent France and Communist China from producing their own nuclear weapons. But with a *détente* the former may become feasible, and it may be possible to limit the destabilizing effect which two new nuclear powers would have on world affairs. In the war machines of East and West there is a strategic interlock: other states might be dragged in when dissidents take action. But if the two nuclear giants have reassured each other beforehand, the peril may be less.

It is difficult at best for each side to provide such assurance. Yet when a few issues are settled, a measure of confidence may be created that would either expedite the settlement of other issues or permit some of these to be bypassed indefinitely. Over certain vexatious questions it will be an agreement to disagree that can do most to promote a *détente.* Whatever is done, both sides will again have to treat disarmament and security – a conjunction that baffled statesmen after World War I – as opposite sides of the same coin.

To work out a durable peace will be as intricate a process as any in which men have ever been collectively engaged. The imperatives of survival must prevail in the end. Using the concept of peace by power, the West has convinced the Soviet Union that peaceful coexistence is preferable to war. Now it must convince the Soviets that peaceful coexistence, Moscow style, does not make for a durable peace. Power for peace exercised by the West has already been persuasive. It should remain our policy until a durable peace has been achieved.

PART THREE

Ambivalence and International Affairs

7 Anti-Nazism and a German Patriot*

Those who handle great issues may or may not do so in terms of personal background. It is this, at any rate, that might have shaped the views of some whom Part Three now discusses.

Adam von Trott zu Solz was never a celebrity though he nearly became one. But a memoir might serve as a reminder of the atmosphere in which during the 1930s the European balance of power was frittered away. The last five years of Trott's life disclosed, moreover, for what, short of total victory by its erstwhile foes, a new German Reich would have negotiated.

Next comes an episode in the career of an American President, Dwight Eisenhower, and John Foster Dulles, his first Secretary of State – two notables who, by misinterpreting the past, made a postwar crisis irreparably worse for the West.

Lastly there is an analysis of Senate testimony by Mr George Kennan, a former diplomatist who, despite his renown as an authority on Russian affairs, seemed unable to distinguish much that was valid in the American past from much that, with the passage of the years, is now utterly invalid.

It is after such preliminaries have also been covered that current problems in the West (those of the 1970s with the 1980s already in sight) can be tackled more directly.

Adam von Trott, a conspirator against Hitler, undertook a transatlantic visit at the dawn of World War II that, if

*This memoir was first published as an article, 'Adam von Trott, Oxford, America and the Anti-Nazis', in the *Spectator* (London, 7 Oct 1972).

About Adam von Trott zu Solz there is a moving narrative by Christopher Sykes, *Troubled Loyalty* (William Collins Sons & Co. Ltd, London, 1968); *Tormented Loyalty* (Harper & Row, New York, 1969).

crowned with success, could only have made it more arduous for Britain to hold out until, two years later, the United States came fully to the rescue. His biographer, Mr Christopher Sykes, has described how the proposals conveyed by Trott were qualified momentarily and then restated. But did anyone in the American or British governments sense at the time all that these might entail?

The ideas purveyed by Trott across the Atlantic were scarcely calculated to fortify the British position. None could have had so dangerous a bearing on Britain's own immediate future. But how familiar are the British people with what was being done in various North American quarters to further the British cause before Pearl Harbour catapulted the United States into war?

There is a rich field to mine quite apart from official policies expressed by President Roosevelt in Lend-Lease, the destroyers for bases deal and the Atlantic Charter. By some political writings of the period, for example, a number of Americans had been made ready psychologically for a switch from isolationism to interventionism, as it were, overnight.

Then, too, it was Trott's sojourn at Oxford which had rendered possible his ventures into personal diplomacy on both sides of the Atlantic. Another look at that may help round out the picture.

Trott failed when the Roosevelt Administration stuck to a looser form of neutrality than he desired. Britain might have collapsed between the fall of France in the spring of 1940 and Pearl Harbour in December 1941 without Lend-Lease, the destroyers-for-bases deal, a morale-booster like the Atlantic Charter. None of these measures would have been feasible if, during the autumn of 1939, Adam von Trott had got his way. Perhaps the Roosevelt Administration would have had to take him more seriously if he himself had had a better grasp of American pressure politics and if Oxford had not been, for a German aristocrat with historic American antecedents of his own, his main ultimate source of introductions to the American scene.

Before this point is developed, it may be well to summarise Trott's general aims. On the eve of the war he had argued at the highest levels in Britain that anti-Nazi elements in the German armed forces could be bribed into revolt against Hitler by letting them retain Nazi conquests. The rulers of Germany were to alter, in other words, but not her overall rule. When these overtures got nowhere, though, there was another decisive factor to be considered by Trott and his seniors in the German Foreign Office. President Woodrow Wilson had thrown the weight of the United States into the scales against the German Empire and it was so as to preserve Germany from a repetition of her ensuing defeat that Trott embarked upon his last voyage across the Atlantic. Generous terms by the Allies, he assured the State Department, were what were likely to hasten the denazification of Germany. These presupposed, if the United States were to serve as a go-between, that she stay neutral and aloof. But what did Trott mean by generous terms? Never was he himself willing to relax the Reich's grip on Austria – though he vacillated, it is true, over the years about other features of German self-aggrandisement. The free world prayed for the Nazi monster to disgorge. To feed the beast was, until the Allies were advancing towards German soil in 1944, Trott's recurrent panacea.

And it is in this context that one unnoticed paradox of Trott's American trip might be suggested. He knew what, for him, were the wrong people. American internationalists whom he had met, directly or indirectly, through his Oxford connections got him in touch with Roosevelt's Washington. But Adam himself must have detected (as some have since confirmed to me) the lack of any real confidence between him and them. There were Americans, all the same, with whom politically he had a lot in common. These were the ones for whom the European hegemony of a larger Reich was less of a menace than co-operative American efforts by which it might be forestalled, curbed or undone.

Nor were they hard to track down. It would have been best for him to avoid Father Coughlin, the Detroit radio personality. Yet there were isolationist militants in the Senate like Messrs Taft, Borah, Wheeler, Nye and Vandenberg: national politicians such as Thomas Dewey, the Republican, and Norman Thomas, the Socialist; so influential a Wall Street apologist for German supremacy as John Foster Dulles. Others also were soon to emerge: the Lindberghs, for whom Nazism was, in their own phrase, the wave of the future; the well-heeled champions of Fortress America, as ex-President Hoover himself dubbed it, and those at Yale who founded America First. Nor could the American Communist Party, non-ideological bedmates of right-wing isolationists, be excluded. A year and a half was to pass, fraught with unprecedented peril for Britain and the free world, before the Nazi-Soviet Pact dissolved into Nazi-Soviet conflict – Communists in the United States, as in Britain and Canada, switching back like automatons to Britain's side. Trott departed from the United States six months before the surrender of France. It had been his business to see the State Department first of all. But his natural allies, powerful isolationist opinion-makers who might have put his case to more adequate use, he seemed to have missed.

Throughout, Adam had been torn between national grievances against the West and ideals he cherished with it. After World War I the 1919 settlement did at least allow for a unified German Reich while it also embodied, for the liberated countries of Eastern Europe, the principle of self-determination. Nowadays the Bonn Republic cannot have the one or urge the other if Ostpolitik is to prevail. But since his Oxford days Trott had been preaching a theory to which Nazis and non-Nazis subscribed – namely, that others and not Germans themselves were responsible for the ills by which their country was beset.

The brief postwar French occupation of the Ruhr, for example, had been child's play as compared with the vast tracts of Belgium and France ravaged by German forces from 1914 to 1918. Postwar inflation, however, had ruined the German middle classes and this was attributed to reparations imposed by the victors under the Treaty of Versailles. Forgotten was the onerous wartime strain the German economy had inflicted upon itself in a war neutral Belgians, at least, did nothing to provoke. Shrugged off, too, were the inflationary methods adopted for evading the payment of reparations by which the vanquished had further impoverished themselves. And during the late 'twenties there was something else that is still ignored. American investment in the German economy surpassed whatever payments Germany did make under 'the servitudes of Versailles'. And so there was another unrecompensed item that brought on the world-wide slump of the 'thirties. Mass unemployment in the lands of the West did not produce Hitlers everywhere. But for resuming the war of 1914-18, Hitler himself could utilize a brand-new industrial plant with which, through unrepaid American investment, the West had endowed the resurgent Germans – a military advantage neither Britain nor France was to enjoy.

The clouds were gathering when Trott arrived at Oxford. To reverse the verdict of 1918 was as much his objective as that of compatriots from whom otherwise he dissented so completely. His dilemma, like that of many in the West, was to shun war while supporting German territorial demands that only war could achieve.

Trott was in his second year at Balliol College and I was in my third when Hitler, on becoming Chancellor, ushered in the Third Reich. With a concept of overriding German claims as advocated by so amiable a zealot as Adam few Oxonians were disposed temperamentally, and fewer equipped intellectually, to quarrel. The West had cardinal interests of its own to preserve. Any counter-assertion of these in Oxford, as elsewhere among the avant-garde of the English-speaking world, generally evoked ridicule.

Lord Lothian, the former Philip Kerr, was then Secretary of the Rhodes Trust and, though he had his headquarters in London, he was, during the early 'thirties, a frequent guest at parties given in Oxford for Rhodes Scholars at Rhodes House. The clue to everything was the friendship that sprang up afterwards between him and Trott as well as between Trott and the parents of David Astor, another Balliol undergraduate, with whom Lothian himself was so close. In those circles the exceptional charm of this dynamic Rhodes Scholar could have been no handicap. But they also shared the same preconceptions on the subject of Germany and without these he might never have got far.

It was a subject, furthermore, over which Lothian, who had been Secretary to Lloyd George at No 10 Downing Street and held ministerial posts in our own day, may have swung from one extreme to the other. On the origins of World War I most Germans, with encouragement from revisionist historians in the West, had always rejected the 'guilt clause' in the Treaty of Versailles. As a draftsman of that clause, Lothian may have been haunted by unadmitted guilt feelings of his own. When he died at the Washington Embassy in December 1940, he had been there a year and a half. A dispassionate study of his record, long overdue, should be done.

As for Trott's friendship with Sir Stafford Cripps, the latter's son, John Cripps, was also with us at Balliol. But in that radical company the emphasis may have been on the domestic sector. About what else, early in the nineteen-thirties, could one who had been Solicitor-General and a dissident member of the Labour Opposition, agree with Adam? Cripps might have concurred that the 1919 settlement was a wrong which still had to be rectified in Germany's favour. And yet if it had been thus rectified the domination of Europe would have passed to Germany without a shot being fired – a state of affairs that could have been countered only by the sort of arms build-up against which the Labour Party clamoured during the nineteen-thirties so insistently. At the Centre there had been Lord Robert Cecil with his peace ballot. For the subsequent plight of the nation, the Conservative Party, having held the reins at Westminster, was the more culpable. Pacifist fervours on the Left were only less to blame.

His Oxford career had thus been the indispensable prelude for activities as unique as Trott's. Without the high-level connections he forged during his two years at Balliol there were political thresholds in Britain and America he could never have crossed, doors he could never have opened.

I was in Toronto when I heard of his trip to the United States during the autumn of 1939. There was nothing political about the postcard that, with others, he sent me from New York. But from Virginia, where he had been at a conference of the Institute for Pacific Relations, Canadian delegates bore further salutations and, when they did so, observed how splendid a job Adam had done for Hitler.

Expediency rather than conviction was, I surmised, what

had impelled him. I had long anticipated his search for leverage against the Nazi regime from a niche within it – these were tactics we had canvassed at Balliol six years before. It was, nevertheless, just as well that I did not go down to New York or Washington during his American pilgrimage and learn that he was seeking a compromise peace which required from the United States the strictest kind of neutrality. I was one of those who long feared that without American intervention all would be lost. After Oxford and during the appeasement years I had lived in London. Before the fall of Austria, when an article of mine had warned against a Nazi-Soviet Pact, I had also written that the United States would be aligned with Britain in any final crisis. In London, too, my book *The Rise of Anglo-American Friendship* had been published two days before Munich and, when an American edition followed, one review not only stated, among other things, that my purpose was to get the United States into the war on the side of Britain, but it appeared (the *American Historical Review*, October 1939) just when Adam arrived to keep her out. This was a coincidence and a profoundly disquieting contrast of which I had no inkling for many years. But it did illustrate, as far as Trott was concerned, that one could be a foe of the Nazis without being an ally of the West.

In this crucial respect Adam might have drawn away, towards the end, from his chief British patron. Necessarily different, at any rate, was Lothian's tone after he went to the Washington Embassy (he visited Toronto on one occasion during that period) from all he had said and done during the preceding decade. It was not until Churchill replaced Chamberlain, as is indicated by papers at the Public Record Office, that the idea of a peace with Hitler himself had been dispelled. Yet neither was Adam's thesis – a compromise peace expedited by an uncompromising American abstention – one that a British envoy in Washington could endorse. There was a secret encounter at the Mayflower Hotel, Washington, between Lothian and his German protégé. With the Gestapo on the prowl, their talk could not be divulged. But Edward Carter, Director of the Institute for Pacific Relations, had arranged the Lothian-Trott rendezvous and, as he soon informed me about it, he must have informed others.

No harm was done. It had been through Lothian himself that, according to Trott's biographer, Adam first met Carter before the war and that a prewar grant from the Rhodes Trust had provided funds for Adam's attendance at the conference of the Institute for Pacific Relations during the autumn of 1939. Not even that meagre British expenditure, in the light of Adam's quest for American neutrality and Britain's own imminent struggle to survive, was devoid of irony.

At once selfless and self-willed, he had striven to exploit Nazism as well as to wipe it out. Eager to save Germany from Hitler he risked everything. But less than eager to save Europe from Germany he had, on that more fundamental issue, leaned towards the Nazis rather than the West.

Were there hints of such ambivalence in Trott before it manifested itself at major turning-points? Symptomatic may be one episode, noted by his biographer, of how he refused to see Churchill when he strove on the eve of the war to elicit the further appeasement of Hitler from Chamberlain and Halifax. Did he exhibit the same schizoid mentality, intellectual escapism tempered later on by the utmost in compassion and courage, during pivotal experiences at Balliol from 1931 to 1933? Minor recollections suggest that he might have done so.

Certainly he was still rather selective in the kind of response he made to critiques of Germany and Germans. 'You Germans are all alike,' I charged with mock-indignation when, from published correspondence, I discovered how, before the 1914 war, German Rhodes Scholars, on getting drunk, threatened British fellow Oxonians with invasion; how the Kaiser had had one sent down after he shot a deer in the lovely park of Magdalen College.* Adam was not amused. Among the offenders may have been Wilhelm von Schweinitz, a Balliol man who was his own uncle. Nor did it please Adam to learn how bellicose in behaviour German undergraduates had been prior to the war of 1914. Such mischief detracted from any assumption of relative German innocence upon which, with most Germans and with so many in the English-speaking world, he predicated the case against

*Stephen Gwynn, ed., *The Letters and Friendships of Sir Cecil Spring Rice* (Constable & Co. Ltd, London, 1930), Vol. II, p. 119.

the 1919 settlement – a line which was to be Trott's own political stock-in-trade until the conspiracy of July 1944 fizzled out and the Nazis hanged him.

Adam covered a lot of ground. He consorted with heads of colleges, dons of all ages and many breeds of undergraduate – Communists of the October Club, younger pillars of the Establishment on the Right, heirs to the anti-Establishment Establishment which had flourished after World War I on the Left. Yet in political discussion two names that should have mattered as much as any to Adam were simply not mentioned in the Sykes biography. They are those of Alfred Zimmern, first occupant of the Oxford Chair in International Relations, a celebrated scholar who conducted a group to which Trott belonged, together with that of Reginald Coupland, Zimmern's counterpart in Commonwealth affairs – an Oxford figure whom Trott must have run across at All Souls and who, as doyen of the Ralegh Club, limited though it was to members from Britain and other Commonwealth countries, exerted much influence upon many generations and types of Oxford men. Zimmern and Coupland had been less well disposed than most of Oxford towards German demands. Trott fell out with A. L. Rowse, another sceptic.

One does not remember, alas, the impression made upon Adam by that notorious episode, also unmentioned by his biographer, when the Oxford Union twice decided that it would not fight for King and Country. Such antics might not have persuaded him, as it may have persuaded Nazis, young and old, that they could defy Britain, still leader of the West, with impunity; his goal always was peace by agreement even if its consequences were more inequitable than the status quo. Nor is there any evidence of how another episode impressed Trott – a conference assembled at Rhodes House between a representative group of Oxford students and a German delegation composed ostensibly of student Nazis.

If it was through Oxford that he got out of his depth, it would have been better for him, in the long run, if he had never gone up. In the short run he gave the University more than it gave him. When Adam waltzed at balls in London as well as Oxford, this tall magnetic creature swept all before him: he would have been a hit even if he had not been a man with a mission. The Commonwealth and American presence had done much, since the turn of the century, to render Oxford less in-grown. But this did not put it socially and intellectually on its mettle. Trott did. For he embodied a degree of upper-class European sophistication that attracted – and even flattered – native British sophisticates, most of humbler birth.

Trott stood out. So did two other German Oxonians of patrician vintage whom Nazi furies consumed. Albrecht von Bernstorff, an older man, was already a friend of Adam's while Helmuth von Moltke organised the resistance group on whose behalf Adam negotiated, during the war, with the West. Bernstorff was still Counsellor of the German Embassy, then on Carlton House Terrace, when, with Count Montgelas, he sat in my rooms at Balliol and warned, seven or eight months before Hitler attained office, of the wrath to come. And those very cottage rooms (now demolished) were the ones in which Trott himself was to dwell during his second year at Oxford.

The resistance group that Adam joined was to rely, for the overthrow of the Nazi regime, on some of the Army High Command and in him the General Staff had had an admirer dating from before the demise of the Weimar Republic – in fact, since the days of General Schleicher. A job on it, Trott remarked to me, was the route to power and, as we sauntered around the garden quadrangle at Balliol, I half expected him to wind up with one.

Nor was this the only way in which he never changed. 'One must have roots,' he used to say to me – a dictum to which may be traced back his rejection of exile because such a move might have jeopardised some he would have left behind.

The Easter vacation of 1933 offered the first opportunity for Adam to see Nazi Germany with his own eyes and for Berthold Krupp, another Balliol contemporary of ours, also to pay it a visit. No two accounts, when they returned, could have been as dissimilar. 'She wept,' was how, according to Trott, his mother received news of early excesses against German Jews. 'She is,' he explained to me, 'a Christian.' Such was the code he inherited and he never hesitated, despite grave hazards, to reaffirm it.

Trott had moral force. But his political ideas were a baffling Hegelian jumble – some derived from the Left, some from the Right, liberal and illiberal, nationalist and internationalist, which he never contrived to sort out. Whenever I teased him about their abstract character he retorted that, as a descendant of John Jay, first Chief Justice of the United States, he also had a stake in the more pragmatic heritage of Anglo-American public affairs. And there, too, a hint of irony might be discerned.

Tradition, at any rate, may be what Adam had in mind when he set sail for the United States upon the outbreak of war. The United States reverted, after 1914-18, to George Washington's counsel against entangling alliances and it was for strict American neutrality that Trott contended during the autumn of 1939. Did he invoke the name of his own eminent American ancestor, an appointee of the first President, when he pleaded at the State Department for the resurrection of outmoded policies? He might well have done so.

The main segment of the West did not mobilise until Japan struck more than two years later. Yet the West had not been wholly self-immobilised and in part that was because, by another wry twist of history, the scion of an old Knickerbocker family, Franklin Delano Roosevelt, acted as he did.

8 The Suez Breach of 1956 and Americans with a Past

Among the might-have-beens of history few can be more tantalising than what the future of the Middle East would have been if the United States under General Eisenhower as President and John Foster Dulles as Secretary of State had let Britain and France restore, according to treaty, an international regime over the Suez Canal.

Israel had just been subjected to her second war with Egypt. Two others, one in 1967 and one in 1973, lay ahead. But in 1956 a Presidential election was also due and General Eisenhower, with Foster Dulles at his elbow, may have felt that more votes might be garnered by rejecting rather than by accepting brief warlike measures.

Abroad the American national interest demanded unison with the chief allies of the United States. Such a necessity had to be shelved if American domestic politics, in most unsoldierly style, were put first.

Below there will be mention of neutralists who might also be won over from Russia – though the White House rebuffed the Kremlin when it imagined that it itself was the one being wooed. But, despite the Anglo-American comradeship of World War II, deeply embedded antipathies rather than new superficial affections might have been what goaded American policymakers.

Pearl Harbour began a new era of American leadership based on Anglo-American friendship and coalition solidarity – axioms that, after the strange interlude of Suez, were to prevail once more. But with General Eisenhower in the White House, each of those who handled the Suez controversy at a high level was, by an odd quirk of fortune, someone who had

* This essay was first published as an article, 'Suez and Americans with a Past', in the *Spectator* (London, 8 May 1971). Book references have been added.

prewar antecedents of an isolationist or anti-British character. And this was a coincidence with which, by his recollections, Harold Macmillan, successor as Prime Minister to Sir Anthony Eden, seemed to be unacquainted.

It was over vehment protests from Sir Winston Churchill that, as Supreme Commander, Eisenhower stopped Allied armies at the Elbe and let the Russians enter Berlin first of all. This, according to documents of the Anglo-American Chiefs of Staff, had been his own military decision. It was one of which memories were to be kept mortifyingly alive as East-West crises over Berlin recurrently flared up. For the step he had taken the General himself blamed President Roosevelt and the meeting with Stalin at Yalta in 1945. A miscalculation that ceded priority to the Soviet Union involved wartime discord with the British directly. More indirect was a preconception that the President betrayed in his war memoirs and which, during the Suez imbroglio, might have been reflected in the activities of his subordinates.

Here an ideological phase of the Suez episode should be recalled. Most anti-colonial countries were neutralists and Dulles, as Secretary of State, had denounced neutralism as immoral. An outmoded colonialism was, all the same, how he dubbed the Suez enterprise. Suddenly, by thus veering away from British and French allies, the United States might even steal a march on the Soviet Union in Afro-Asian quarters. This was a development for which the American people themselves were not prepared. But *Crusade in Europe,* a 1948 volume of reminiscences by General Eisenhower, could have afforded a glimpse into the mentality that, during 1956-57, was to rock the West and expedite the Soviet grip on the Middle East. Discussing relations between the United States and Russia, Eisenhower remarked that 'both were free from the stigma of colonial empire-building by force'.* Britain and France might be pillars of the West. They were, by contrast, scarcely free from any such stigma.

*So historically ill-informed an opinion about ruthless expansion by Tsarist Russia and the Soviet Union, as well as by the United States herself, came to light in a volume published three years after World War II had terminated and when the cold war had begun. (Doubleday & Co. Inc., Garden City, N.Y., 1948) p. 457.

Did so politically illiterate a credo yield a telltale clue to the General's emotional reflexes during the Suez venture? It is anybody's guess. In the Middle East the residual position of the West had been undermined when the Sixth Fleet was misused, Britain also coerced through pressure on the pound, the Western Alliance demoralised and American pledges to Israel violated unhesitatingly. There had been no such windfall for the Soviet Union since it spread its rule from the Baltic through Eastern Europe to the Balkans. And at present, with NATO members so eager to have the Suez Canal unblocked when the West is challenged globally by Russian sea power, Moscow can only await other strategic gifts on the same cosmic scale.

But whatever the shape of things to come in the Middle East, none did more to remould them during the 'fifties than John Foster Dulles. Before the Anglo-American divergence over Suez, he had disagreed with Sir Anthony Eden about the Far East. And they differed in emphasis even when they concurred that Nasser should not get away with the nationalisation of the Suez Canal. Sir Anthony Eden, renowned as a prewar foe of appeasement, warned against a repetition of prewar mistakes; the less Dulles heard about prewar mistakes the more content he was likely to be. For when, with Churchill, Eden sounded the alarm against Axis dictatorships, John Foster Dulles had been finding excuses for them.

These, at any rate, would have been the beneficiaries of that 'peaceful change' which, in his writings, Dulles urged the West to accept. What he portrayed between the wars as 'dynamic' forces were, during the years of America First, to be hailed by Lindbergh as 'waves of the future' (until, that is, December 1941 when Pearl Harbour demonstrated how the United States herself might be engulfed). After Munich, as late as Hitler's prewar seizure of Prague, John Foster Dulles, in an address at the Economic Club of New York (22 March 1939), scoffed at the notion that the defense of the United States might be bound up with the defense of free peoples elsewhere. So immune was she, he declared, that only hysteria could entertain the idea of Germany, Italy or Japan contemplating war upon her. What worried Dulles was not Axis domination but any American participation in the coming war that merely restored the 'military domination' of Britain and France. To maintain the European preponderance of the British and French was, as Dulles saw it, to prolong injustice. Justice would be done, in other words, when their power crumbled – a contingency upon which Nazi warlords might have looked without demur.

Nor was that all. Before Pearl Harbour, when President Franklin Delano Roosevelt still had to combat isolationist sentiment in devising the bases-for-destroyers deal, he welcomed support from a round-robin of eminent American lawyers which John Foster Dulles refused to sign. The story is that Dulles, among others, said Britain was finished. But if so, did he oppose the measure lest it offend the presumed Nazi victors with whom, if Britain fell, serious public business might soon have to be done? That would have been consonant with the views Dulles voiced on the eve of the war; from them, in retrospect, a collaborationist potential cannot be excluded. Dulles was one of those, a type familiar on both sides of the Atlantic, who acquire an unshakable reputation for integrity or even wisdom when a certain technical competence is what they mostly exhibit. After Pearl Harbour he represented the Republican party in bipartisan endeavours. As the international situation changed it was expedient for him, over the years, also to change his mind. His behaviour during the Suez episode suggested, nevertheless, that since the 'thirties and 'forties some of his deepest political instincts, as distinguished from the new problems of a new age, had not really altered. And by these he himself might have been taken unawares.

Afterwards, moreover, Eisenhower and Dulles asked British visitors associated with Eden (later, the Earl of Avon) why he had called a halt to the Suez venture prematurely. But the damage had been done and their feigned solicitude only added insult to injury.

Then there was the antagonism displayed at the United Nations by Henry Cabot Lodge Jr and, as Number Two at the State Department, by Herbert Hoover Jr. It may or may not be significant that, as young men, both had been isolationists. As luck would have it, each of them also cherished family loyalties that may have coloured personal initiatives during the Anglo-American divergence over Suez.

Nobody had known that Henry Cabot Lodge Jr was so devoted to the United Nations, and for this unexpected ardour two explanations reached London. The indications were, however, that the first of these was entirely incorrect while the second, if half right, was also half wrong.*

The younger Lodge did not manifest the slightest desire to make amends for damage wrought after World War I by his grandfather; he never acknowledged that any damage had been done. The elder Lodge, it will be remembered, operated as the spearhead for Senators who prevented the United States from redeeming a security pledge made by President Woodrow Wilson to war-ravaged France and from ratifying, with the Treaty of Versailles, the Covenant of the League of Nations. But as recently as 1953 – three years, that is, before the Suez venture – the younger Lodge had denied in notes added by him to a biography of his grandfather that the elder Lodge had ever ill-served the cause of peace.

Anglophobia did no doubt inspire Henry Cabot Lodge Jr. But this was not typical of Boston as a whole. Most of its intellectual élite, from Emerson to Henry Adams, had long swung back. But it is true that, as a group, the Lodges had not forgotten 1776. Among confidants of President Theodore Roosevelt, Lodge the elder had been the most belligerent when negotiations were on foot to demarcate the boundaries of Alaska with northern Canada; no other item, in Britain's effort to settle outstanding disputes with the United States, was as thorny. At the turn of the century a German bid for naval supremacy threatened the *Pax Britannica*, an oceanic system without which the United States herself might not have been safe, and an Anglo-American factor emerged as the pre-1914 realignment of the powers was hammered out. None did more to impede the emergence of that Anglo-American factor than Senator Henry Cabot Lodge, an American public man to whom the younger Lodge owed his

*The reports about Lodge that reached London were noted by Harold Macmillan, successor as Prime Minister to the Earl of Avon (Sir Anthony Eden), in *Riding the Storm 1956-1959* (Macmillan, London, 1971) pp. 151-2.

upbringing. It was in the spirit of one particular clan and not of their native city that, during the Anglo-American divergence over Suez, the American representative at the United Nations expressed himself.

And as with the Lodges, so with the Hoovers. Fortress America had been the isolationist vision of Herbert Hoover as President and, while his son may not have subscribed to it, there were those in the Senate, fellow Republicans, who thought he did. Beyond filial piety was the outlook of an American oil engineer for whom the protection of American oil investments might bulk large. Only two years before the Anglo-American divergence over Suez, at any rate, Herbert Hoover Jr, had been deemed anti-British when, after the Mossadegh nationalisation of British oil property, he negotiated the Iranian oil consortium. And it was he who, as Acting Secretary of State, did most, through oil sanctions, to tighten the screws on the transatlantic allies of the United States at the time of Suez.*

But be that as it may, Russia had everything to gain in 1956-57 and nothing to lose, from hidden, private, unsuspected tensions among the makers and executants of American policy. The most inadvertent reminders of their buried political past are not relished by any who have had misjudgements of their own to live down. And those, American or British, who have misjudged great issues in one era must beware lest, if they get the chance, they misjudge them in yet another.

Nor was this the end of the affair. A strange light was shed on the high-flown pieties of Messrs Eisenhower and Dulles in 1956-7 when Anglo-American landings were made in the Lebanon and Jordan during the summer of 1958. By the time of that unabashed turnabout, however, a new era had begun. Against Soviet penetration of the Middle East, with all that might ensue, there was left, with Turkey, Iran and Israel, only the American Sixth Fleet.

*Most of the material for this essay was drawn from Lionel Gelber, *America in Britain's Place* (New York and London, 1961) pp. 212-91.

9 The Politics of Nostalgia*

There may be unwitting segments of American opinion that believe the United States could backtrack and go it alone, but this is not a view that a celebrated specialist is expected, during an era of global politics and American leadership, wishfully to express. Mr George Kennan did so, all the same, in hearings before the Senate Committee on Foreign Relations, 1966 and 1967.

Few, if any, of the major American opinion media pronounced upon such an exercise in the politics of nostalgia. An account, extracted from a longer article, is reprinted here.

It was a prewar British historian, H. A. L. Fisher, who, in the preface to his *History of Europe,* told us that the play of the contingent and unforeseen is the only safe rule for the historian to observe. But his timing was poor. There was nothing unforeseen about the dread consequences of the appeasement line then being pursued by his own country — with the blessing, be it noted, of British historians as renowned as Arnold Toynbee and E. H. Carr. History may be studied for a number of reasons. Its value is academic, or even antiquarian, if, among current perplexities, it does not help us to find the way ahead.

Skepticism about its utility on this score has been propounded by an outstanding American historian, Arthur Schlesinger, Jr. To depend on history for guidance in the short run at least may, he feels, do more harm than good. But one is puzzled when Schlesinger points to the Nazi-Soviet pact as a pivotal event which could not be foreseen.†

*This essay was first published as an article, 'History and The American Role', in *Orbis* (Spring 1967). Much of the first half has been deleted and there have been minor corrections.

†Arthur M. Schlesinger, Jr, *The Bitter Heritage* (Houghton Mifflin, Boston, 1967) p. 99.

On whether or not the Nazi-Soviet Pact could have been foreseen the reader, by turning back to Chapter 1 of this book, can judge for himself.

And yet if it is true that, as Pascal said, to govern is to foresee, even the best of representative democracies have been sadly misgoverned. Officeholders cannot pry into the future when they take their cue from what the public wants rather than from realities of which the people should be, but are not, steadily apprised. History, all the same, may induce the far-sighted to look where the imprescient never glance. It must not be downgraded, in other words, when the fault lies elsewhere. Those who follow beaten paths can dispense with history as a beacon. It may, nevertheless, prompt voices that cry in the wilderness and to some of which heed might still be paid.

War recurred in 1939 because lessons taught by the war of 1914-1918 had been ignored. Why did this happen? Wishfulness had much to do with appeasement in Britain between the wars and with its transatlantic counterpart, the isolationism into which the United States relapsed after 1918. But there were also those who made it their business to capitalize on such folly. Distorting the supreme issues of the age, they shook the faith of free societies in the moral validity of their own cause.

After World War II, however, it was in the light of prewar errors that the West resolved, under the American lead, to do better. On some fronts that reading of history has paid off. Would it do so on others?

This was a vital question at a juncture when American intervention in Viet Nam had stirred up another great debate on the character of American commitments abroad. In that debate, the hearings held in 1966 and again in 1967 by the Senate Committee on Foreign Relations were a forum for responsible criticism of American policy. Senator J. William Fulbright, chairman of the Senate Foreign Relations Committee, set the tone of the hearings, and on both occasions former Ambassador George F. Kennan appeared as a witness. His testimony coincided with opinions expressed by the Senator.

Both men urged the American people to adopt a less wide-ranging concept of the American role, and to drive their point home they armed themselves with the evidence of history. Though Senator Fulbright was not a professional historian, he had made his mark as an intellectual; George Kennan's writings on Russian history brought him considerable acclaim. Yet history is a two-edged sword. As a weapon in America's great debate, it should have been wielded with care.

And it was with the Senator's concurrence that Kennan, at the 1966 hearings, submitted an 'historical' solution of his own, namely, that countries such as the two Viet Nams should adapt themselves to the new China as Yugoslavia adapted herself to Soviet Russia in the postwar era.

But here, peculiarly enough, was the kind of historical analogy Fulbright and Kennan condemned the Johnson Administration for invoking. Yugoslavia is, after all, within the strategic ambit of the West; between her land frontiers and those of the Soviet Union there is no contact.* Geography does not permit the neighbours of China to cut themselves off from the Chinese imperium with the same ease should they, impelled by their own sense of nationhood, want to rebel. Perhaps in domestic affairs they could achieve some Titoist modifications. But in every other respect the domination of China would be consolidated inexorably over large tracts of Asia.

That may ensue anyway. An attempt to avert it might still be made, provided more Asian countries like Tibet are not now abandoned to Chinese hegemony. It is extraordinary how a solution so utterly at variance with liberal tenets should have come to gain credit with liberals. It used to be a liberal aim to preserve the independence of small countries. Now official American endeavours in this respect were stigmatised by liberals as illiberal. And in such a muddle there was also something reminiscent of prewar trends. British intellectuals are apt to forget how much appeasement on the Right borrowed from the Centre and the Left between the

*Even so there was to be less composure about the future of Yugoslavia and the Mediterranean presence of the Soviet Union as the demise of Tito, the Yugoslav dictator, loomed up.

wars. American isolationists were drawn from the ranks of liberals as well as conservatives.

Two passages from the testimony Kennan gave in 1966 were singularly anachronistic. He began by quoting as pertinent a statement from John Quincy Adams, as though rhetoric suited to the world of 1821 had some bearing on global tasks which, *faute de mieux,* the United States has had to shoulder in the second half of the twentieth century. The United States, Adams had declared, 'is the well-wisher to the freedom and independence of all. She is the champion and vindicator only of her own.' But has not so oversimplified a summary been out of date ever since the Pax Britannica broke down? The United States can be the champion and vindicator of her own freedom only by being the champion and vindicator of freedom on a much larger scale. It took two world wars to teach her this lesson, and their sequel, the East-West contest, made it no less cogent. These are the commonplaces of history in the modern era. They were, all the same, overlooked.

But others, too, overlooked what Kennan was driving at. He did not warn, in the words of George Washington and Thomas Jefferson, against permanent and entangling alliances. But he confessed to having 'more and more sympathy for the concepts of foreign policy that prevailed in this country at an earlier time, and I find myself, if you will, in many respects sort of a neo-isolationist'.*

It is disconcerting that virtual silence should have greeted an admission of neo-isolationism from a public man so influential as George Kennan. One explanation for the immunity Kennan enjoyed may be that with every backward step he also took a step forward. 'We have,' he hastened to add, 'an enormous responsibility with regard to world peace.' A preference for neo-isolationism, in other words, would not blind

*This significant passage from Kennan's testimony did not appear in *The Vietnam Hearings* (Random House, New York, 1966), a report of the proceedings for which ex-Senator Fulbright wrote an introduction. It will be found in U.S. Congress, Senate, Committee on Foreign Relations, *Hearings, Supplemental Foreign Assistance FY 1966 – Vietnam,* 89th Congress, 2nd Session, p. 386. For the quotation from John Quincy Adams, see p. 336.

him to the realities of power. Yet how should we deal with those realities? Some Americans may be searching for a compromise between a parochialism discredited by history and a global leadership which in Kennan's opinion (and in the opinion of Walter Lippmann) has been overdone. But has it, by and large, been overdone? There is no visible alternative to it, despite the imperfections that must attend so vast an enterprise.

Nobody will quarrel with Kennan's further contention that, in preserving peace, the United States can contribute most toward a peace among the Great Powers. How could they? In 1966, nevertheless, as he veered and tacked with his own historical analogies, the neo-isolationist vein persisted.

Neo-isolationism would be at odds with Maxim Litvinoff's famous postulate, that peace is indivisible. That must be why, when he testified before the Senate Committee in both 1966 and 1967, Kennan assailed with such vehemence the prewar dictum of the most pro-Western of Soviet statesmen.* But Kennan could scarcely rewrite the history of the twentieth century because of his dissent from what the United States has done or may do in one area, peripheral or decisive as the case may be.

Ever since Sarajevo in 1914 it has been through local conflicts that world conflicts, long in the making, have come to a head. Many millions were to die for Danzig. In some local conflicts, intervention from afar may be neither practicable nor necessary, and these can be permitted to take their course. Others, such as the invasion of South Korea in 1950, could be localized because the United States intervened at once. But the situation which constrains her to intervene is not always one of local conflict. During the Cuban missile crisis of 1962, the sinister accord between the Soviets and Cubans provoked an American response that, by preserving the global balance, had an impact that was more than local. The contingencies with which the United States must cope may vary. No prior curb can be put on her capacity to meet them, with or without the support of allies.

Litvinoff knew what he was talking about. When all is so explosively interconnected, peace is more indivisible than

*Ibid., p. 386; *Hearing* (1967) op. cit., p. 56.

ever. The United States now has a global balance to maintain. It cannot be maintained if there is that narrowing of scope for which Kennan has hankered.

When Kennan testified before the Senate Committee in 1967, he seemed less disposed to turn the clock back than he had been in 1966. He did not again dub himself a neo-isolationist when Senator Clifford P. Case brought up that point. But he did repeat the quotation he had culled from John Quincy Adams and again attributed to it the same curious, outmoded relevance.*

This was a bewildering performance by one to whose expression of views a unique authority is apt to be attached. And yet there has long been something enigmatic about the counsel Kennan had tendered. 'Containment' is the word he employed when, at the State Department, it was his job to clarify postwar American policy toward the Soviet Union. Conditions in Asia are not the same. Resistance to China, if China is to be resisted, may have to take other forms. But did Kennan fully perceive all that containment entailed? There are grounds for doubt. The Truman Doctrine of 1947, with its offer of Greek-Turkish aid, was the classic exposition of containment – the Marshall Plan and the North Atlantic Alliance grew out of it. Yet among American officials, according to an 'inside' account, George Kennan happened to be the one who, when the Truman Doctrine was being drafted, opposed it most strenuously. Kennan also insisted upon restricting the North Atlantic Alliance to a political guarantee when the need for a more concrete buildup first arose.†

Two decades passed before Kennan's own memoirs confirmed this point. And it seems as intellectually perverse today as it did when first adopted after the ordeal of prewar, wartime and postwar Europe. In 1948-9, according to Kennan, the danger was political rather than military. ‡

**Hearing* (1967) op. cit., p. 57.

†Joseph M. Jones, *The Fifteen Weeks* (The Viking Press, New York, 1955) pp. 154-5.

‡George F. Kennan, *Memoirs 1925-1950* (Hutchinson, London, 1968) pp. 397-414.

No such dichotomy made sense. In Eastern Europe the fact or threat of Russian military occupation is what shored up governance by minions of local Communist parties. It was to this that Jan Masaryk's tragic fate had been attributed. And so the liberators of Western Europe provided against all contingencies. There might have been no economic recovery, as stimulated by the Marshall Plan, if it did not have the North Atlantic Alliance as a military shield.

It was curious, all the same, that Truman and Acheson turned down Kennan's advice just when so many publicists were praising him for a wisdom by which the highest echelons of government were pervaded.

Containment, as a matter of fact, was but another label for concepts of peace by power. A few political realists had been giving shape to these for nearly a decade before the American government, faced with the Soviet Union's postwar intransigence and Britain's recessional, picked them up in 1947.

The new realists, as they exposed prewar errors and forecast postwar realities, might have paved the way for containment. What counted most, of course, was the direct experience of Churchill, Roosevelt and Truman. It will be for the historian of containment to depict its complex origins and to identify those upon whom President Truman leaned for counsel. But when Kennan confessed that he was now a 'sort of neo-isolationist', had he changed his mind or, while spelling out policies of another character, had he always been one?

What conclusions may we derive from this phase of America's great debate? Hearings before a Committee of the Senate are not the kind of data to which theologians or philosophers normally resort when they ponder the meaning of history. But proceedings such as these have affected policies on which the well-being of civilized society depends. They must therefore be taken seriously.

Those who invoke history would do well to remember how history, when misused, can itself be a source of misjudgment. It is the custom nowadays to affirm or controvert the relevance of a term like 'Munich' when an accommodation between Washington and Hanoi or Peking is discussed. But for a more complete grasp of that term we must recall the moral and political atmosphere of the epoch to which it belonged.

Appeasement in Britain and isolationism in the United States nourished each other. Yet they owed a lot to some writers whose misinterpretations of recent history helped to demoralize free peoples at a moment when the West, by closing ranks, could have stopped Hitler in time. On both sides of the Atlantic there were those who gave preparedness a bad name by blaming munition-makers for stirring up threats to peace when their provenance was so much more deep-seated. Then, too, there was a school of revisionist historians who, as apologists for the pre-1914 brand of German militarism, gave appeasement its rationale and lent even to Hitler's culminating mania an air of plausibility.

Chamberlain, after all, was no innovator; he was an end product. And for activities of which 'Munich' was the outcome, the intellectually culpable have never had to answer.

Men may differ over what history has to teach and over what its use might be. But it can, by putting major issues in perspective, show the way. And if it does that a number of pitfalls may be avoided.

PART FOUR

The West and its Compulsive Infelicities

10 Coalition Diplomacy – Early Allied Critiques of American Postwar Leadership*

In one respect the major postwar alignments have resembled each other. Among none has leadership been easy. There is no comparison, however, between the voluntary origins of the North Atlantic Alliance and the involuntary ones of the Warsaw Pact. Afterwards, too, when the West Europeans demanded equality, it was with the two superpowers and not just with the United States. So also when China broke away from Russia she had territorial grievances to make the pan-Communist schism more acrimonious.

But little of that had supervened as yet and since the winter of 1953-4, when this analysis was first published, global politics have been transmuted. The politico-strategic outlook is, as a result, very different for the West. And it calls for a very different sort of approach.

Europe has been railing against Americanization since the 1920s. But this hitherto was visualized as American influence on folkways and popular culture – from the movies to the consumption of Coca-Cola. In the epoch of Senator McCarthy a more serious note is struck. For Europeans either overestimate his grip on the liberties of the country or underestimate that pro-Soviet conspiracy out of which – liberals having pooh-poohed it – he made capital. McCarthyism has an impact which confirms, as it heightens, a concept of America that antedates Senator Joseph McCarthy and may outlast him. At rock bottom, in reacting against Americanization, Europeans have been fleeing from realities which are inherent in the twentieth century itself. The United States is the chief exemplar of mass production; to retain its freedom

*This essay was first published as an article, 'The Diplomacy of Leadership', in the *Antioch Review* Vol. XIII, No. 4 (Yellow Springs, Ohio, Winter 1953-4); reprinted by permission of the editors. It has been slightly reduced in length.

in the modern contest of large-scale entities, Western Europe may have to transform its economy on the American model. And since they prefer old traditions to new exigencies, West Europeans decry that symbol of bigness which is America.

Between themselves, nevertheless, six West European countries soon dismantled obstacles to bigness in trade.

But the problem is not solely one of Western Europeans accepting with good grace the social consequences of large-scale organization. They are tied, for their own safety, to the might of the American colossus. Yet they are loath sometimes to adopt measures urged upon them by the United States. And while these may be rejected on their merits, such reluctance also springs from the manner in which they are put forward. As she leads the Grand Coalition of the free, the United States must perceive that conventional diplomacy is not enough; that the diplomacy of leadership calls for qualities of tact and insight as unprecedented as the conditions for which they must be geared.

It was a Cambridge don, Professor Denis Brogan, who, in a brilliant phrase came nearest to explaining the American temper. He traces it to the illusion of American omnipotence – the belief, when matters abroad go amiss, that it is not their intractibility which is to blame but, since nothing is beyond the capacity of the United States, treason or knavery at home. It is from this angle that Americans look upon the fall of China to Mao tse-Tung. It is submitted here, however, that Brogan's illuminating exposition is, as it stands, somewhat incomplete; he has, as it were, told only half the story. For there are two illusions of the same species involved; and the second, which derives from the first, is the illusion of American omniscience. By the former the potentialities of American control over hostile forces are exaggerated; by the latter it is the susceptibilities of America's own friends and allies which may, at awkward moments, be ignored.

If the sagacity of the United States in foreign affairs matched her strength, the illusion of American omniscience would be no illusion. But does it? That she can do more than her partners is true; that she knows better than they what should be done has been more doubtful. And her assumption is of very recent vintage. It takes for granted that good judgment dawned overnight with primacy. The United States rose to world power under McKinley; but from the days of the first Roosevelt to those of the second, the American people, except for the interlude of World War I, would not recognize the extent of their own stake in the preservation of our free world order. If membership in the United Nations, if the Truman Doctrine, the Marshall Plan, NATO and mutual aid, security pacts with Pacific and Latin American countries have been a valid contemporary approach, then, by their mere existence, they impugn a previous generation which spurned such undertakings. These, moreover, are all co-operative endeavors and it is as such that they must be handled. The paymaster as he pays the piper may feel that he ought to call the tune. But for harmony in his own camp he should not be tone-deaf.

Public utterances which show little respect for the spirit of coalition diplomacy will not enhance respect for America herself. And when American membership in the United Nations, when the future of the United Nations itself, would hinge on China's seat, that is letting a lesser issue – whatever its rights or wrongs – determine a greater. To throw out the baby with the bath water is to take, in the name of morality, a course that is not even sound morally. Nor is there a consistency on moral issues among American politicians which will impress non-Americans. If China is an aggressor – and she is – is Franco Spain innocent of official crime? Yet the United States may enter into an agreement with the latter while striving to debar the former, after Korean hostilities cease, from the international body. Such alternations of principle debase principle. They imply, moreover, that whatever the United States does is right because she does it. And a mood of that kind, when she deals with partners who are as morally aware as herself, could ruin any coalition.

But it is not only Senators, with their potent voice in working out American foreign policy, who may put up the backs of America's allies. The Executive branch have also been impelled by the illusion of American omniscience; have, under Democrats and Republicans alike, been headstrong in trying to impose their will on their own associates. Under both parties the American government has, since World War II, been too intent upon international co-operation for it to threaten a reversal of major trends when these cannot always be accelerated at the speed or in the manner desired – even though Mr Dulles, on his first visit to Europe after taking over the State Department, appeared to be on the verge of doing just this. 'We know,' he himself later asserted before the eighth General Assembly of the United Nations, 'that we have no monopoly of wisdom or virtue.' But how well is that known? For the significant thing about this remark was that the Secretary of State addressed it to the allies rather than the foes of the United States, that American coalition diplomacy in Europe and Asia had reached a pass in which such a statement could be delayed no longer.

Nor did this deter Senator McCarthy who, in his quest for conformity on trade with China, would resort to economic coercion within the camp of the West itself. Talk of that kind the White House and the State Department were bound to repudiate. Yet unless the European Defence Community is ratified, Mr Dulles himself now warns, there will be 'an agonizing reappraisal' of Washington's European course.

France rejected the proposal and there was no American reappraisal, agonising or painless. These lines were published, it may also be recalled, before General de Gaulle returned to office.

The military implications of so grave an intra-allied threat may not be clear. As Atlantic coalition diplomacy it was but another example of *gaucheries* which undo with one hand the good done by the United States with the other.

The French, to go back a few years, have, for instance, never quite recovered from the shock inflicted by Mr Acheson in the autumn of 1950 when, without prior notice, he demanded the rearmament of the new West German Republic. Unison with Britain and France in German affairs had hitherto been the ABC of American postwar policy. It was they and not the United States who were twice maimed in one lifetime by Teutonic aggressions. The principal allies of the United States are neither suppliants nor satellites. Morally they enjoy a perfect right to be consulted by the leader of the Western coalition before any major departure in their joint efforts is broached. Intellectually their national experience must equip them with a comprehension of the German problem which surpasses that of Americans who have, on the highest levels, dealt with it. Potsdam, through a series of improvisations evoked by Soviet ill-will, had been undermined. The West European allies of the United States realized that Mr Acheson's insistence was a logical conclusion to the establishment of the Bonn Republic and to the revival of the Ruhr's heavy industry – that bedrock of German intransigence in aims and arms. Yet here was omniscience taking it upon itself to force the pace, to know best complexities and subtleties for which it was prepared by nothing in the American record or the American situation.

At a time when West Germans are lacking in militancy and have voted in large numbers for a Western orientation under Chancellor Adenauer it is, nevertheless, American self-assurance rather than Gallic forebodings which seem to have been vindicated. But Stresemann was not immortal and neither is Adenauer. The material foundations of German power have been restored; used in accordance with one tendency today, they can be used in accordance with another tomorrow. Perhaps the West German Republic should be rearmed. It may be that a Slavonic onslaught cannot be countered locally without twelve German divisions.

Washington might have been less abrupt if, globally, it was not torn between two diverse zones. During the Korean War it could not let a rival camp take advantage in Europe of American preoccupations elsewhere.

Most of what the Germans want for the fulfilment of ultimate national ambitions lies beyond the grasp of the West and within the orbit of the Soviet Union. And this is a brute fact which American policy makers have side-stepped. What the United States had to give the Bonn Republic has virtually been given; soon the West Germans can be wholly on their own. Soon, too, the heirs of Adenauer, thanks to assistance thus received, will be able to negotiate with Russia from strength; no Balkan puppets, they could be more independent than Mao tse-Tung. Washington and Bonn may hope otherwise. But as long as the Communist regime is on top in Russia it will not ever really abandon Eastern Europe; in an era of East-West deadlock, it is therefore only by linking up with the Soviet Union that the West Germans may repossess land, brethren and trading opportunities which would return to them again their place in the sun.

The German Right, in tune with rooted tradition, has always been aware of this. When the Social Democrats oppose the entry of the Bonn Republic into the European Defence Community, they keep open the way for German unity on Russian terms. Can so dire a contingency be prevented by any federalizing device which would recast the politics and productive forces of Western Europe? It is one of those risks that are more incalculable than calculated. In the eyes of Washington the French might be unduly apprehensive; but in the eyes of Paris the Americans, for all their vaunted realism, have not yet grappled with the inmost European realities. As expedients to canalize that Germanic dynamism which Mr Acheson was so eager to release, the French invented both the Schuman Plan and the European Defence Community; but while expending blood and treasure in Indo-China and while holding North Africa for NATO, they may, on second thoughts, have wished the West European coal-steel pool to succeed before plunging ahead with a European Army which entails German rearmament. Nor, in this context, did the uprising of East Germans against Russian overlords on June 17, 1953, prove that all Germans will march inevitably with the West. It may only have demonstrated that against a foreign yoke – as from Jena to the 1920s – Germans always rebel.

French misgivings over the contents of American policy in Germany have thus been accentuated by the rush in which it was pushed through. Nor is it only the aggrandizement of West Germany itself which causes worry. West Europeans suspect that the United States may inadvertently facilitate German mastery by leaving them to face it alone. Even if there were no more Bismarcks, no more Rapallos, no more Nazi-Soviet pacts, even if a resurgent Germany could be counted on to cling loyally to a European Defence Community, such a project may presage a weakening rather than a strengthening of the West. For its underlying postulate might turn out, from the American standpoint, to be a neo-isolationist one.

Omniscient about what others should do, Americans themselves are still far from clear about the scope and duration of their own permanent responsibilities. Germany in two world wars demolished irretrievably the European balance of power; peace is maintained in the global arena by an American-Soviet equilibrium. European allies of the United States and Canada may, if steadily underpinned, be a very substantial regional adjunct of this new global equipoise. Yet the risk of a remilitarized Germany is to be taken on three hypotheses, resting on continental rather than transatlantic power, which are either obsolete, naive, or ominous. Of these the first would presuppose that Europe's own balance of power can somehow be set up by itself once more. The second is the premise that within it a nationally resurrected Germany will observe with fidelity the restraints of a European Defence Community. And the third is that, as a result of all this, the United States may be able to disengage her own land forces from Western Europe, from a vital sector of the global balance. Such a European policy might contrast with that pursued in Korea, or indeed elsewhere on the Pacific, where the United States has been undertaking fresh obligations; in the light of other British and French commitments it would be tantamount to putting on Germany the onus of European defence. What nourishes it, in brief, is the conviction that the historically uncontrollable can, on the mere American say-so, yet be controlled. And it is anxieties thus stirred up which predispose West Europeans to look with less skepticism than Americans on conciliatory gestures by Moscow.

The British now agree with the United States on the role of Germany in the defense of the West and are willing to go as far as other interests allow to reassure the French. Nevertheless when the British balked at joining the Schuman Plan, American censure revealed Washington again exhorting others to take steps of whose full consequence it had small inkling. What the European Defence Community is expected to accomplish in its sphere, the Schuman Plan had been designed to do in the realm of basic resources: to absorb German energies, as fostered by the United States, in some larger grouping. And taken together all such ideas (excellent in themselves) point to a European federal union – whether it be founded on a coal-steel pool, a West European Army, a West European Parliament (as distinguished from the Council of Europe) or some blend of the three.

Then there is the question of India and the Korean peace-making. Neutral in the East-West struggle and yet a member of the Commonwealth, India's position as a go-between has been unique. To win her goodwill, to expedite her good offices, is to further the American aim of keeping free Asia outside the Sino-Soviet bloc. Yet both Mr Acheson and Mr Dulles were, at unexpected junctures, to rub India the wrong way; and, on both occasions, other Powers of the Commonwealth, so as to hold open the bridge between New Delhi and Washington, had to talk back bluntly to their American ally. In December, 1952 Britain and Canada were astonished to discover that the United States would not endorse India's proposal for the repatriation of Korean prisoners of war. In the end the United States forebore; eventually it was this proposal upon which the Korean truce would be negotiated – with India herself becoming chairman of the Neutral Nations Repatriation Commission. Yet in August, 1953, Mr Dulles having taken over at the State Department from Mr Acheson, there occurred a similar episode – one which was bound to offend the Indians once more. Only five days before the General Assembly reconvened to select participants for the Korean political conference, Britain and Canada were again dismayed to hear that the United States would not support India. There had been no private forewarning, as between friends and allies, through the channels of diplomacy; this time, moreover, Washington did not relent. Later, when she voted for the election of Mrs Pandit to succeed Lester Pearson of Canada as the next President of the General Assembly, the United States tried lamely to make amends. But the most cogent of cases can be spoiled – (there was much to be said for and against the attendance of India) – by shock tactics. And in a coalition of equals such tactics could be fatal.

A mixture of impatience and infallibility – as the atmosphere in capitals as well-disposed as London and Ottawa would indicate – will not enhance American leadership. For if omniscience is unilateral, co-operation is multilateral and too much of the one might undo a lot of the other.

It is from history itself that we must learn where analogies from history no longer apply. The illusion of American omnipotence, Brogan argued, is an improvement on the arrogance displayed by the British during their Victorian heyday. But the British, under the easier circumstances of the earlier era, enjoyed a latitude in foreign affairs which terminated with the nineteenth century itself. Economically and strategically American luck has been superior to that of all other Great Powers. Diplomatically the United States had the misfortune to come of age in a more dangerous epoch. Three times, it is true, her intervention turned the scales – in 1917-18; in 1941-45; and by her current internationalism. But it was Britain and France who held the fort from 1914 to 1917 until the United States was ready and at an irreparable cost to themselves; it was Britain, with support from other Commonwealth countries, who repeated that performance after the fall of France until Russia had been assailed and until Pearl Harbor had roused the American giant from his torpor. Nothing the United States has done – and she has done much – can yet, by any comparative reckoning, equal the sacrifices of the French and British to save, during its darkest hours, our free world order. Efforts which sapped the vigor of France and reduced Britain's world rank have served but to raise America – and Canada – in both vigor and rank. The cause which was common in wartime is still a common one.

And so the global task of the United States varies from that once discharged by Britain as the nineteenth century varied from the twentieth. When the British were supreme, their predominance was such that, except for a transient phase like the Crimean War, they had no need of allies. They did not even have to be friendly with the United States – even though it was the *Pax Britannica* which protected that country (and put teeth into the Monroe Doctrine) during formative years of growth, civil war and expansive post-bellum self-preoccupation. Nevertheless when Salisbury, the last of the Victorian Prime Ministers, spoke of splendid isolation it had already ceased to be splendid. An Anglo-American factor, arrangements with Japan, France and Tsarist Russia ushered in a new era. In her greatest days, however, Britain did not have to pursue, as a fixed feature of policy, a coalition diplomacy. For the United States, if she is to stay at the summit of global power, there is no alternative to one.

It is to nations which groan under a Russian yoke that allied complaints against American leadership might be least intelligible. For the proof of freedom regained would be that any kind of complaint can be uttered with impunity. Dislike of the United States may resemble dislike of Britain, when she exercised paramount power, yesterday. But it was not until the end of the nineteenth century, when others attempted to combine against Britain, that Anglophobia was translated into a common policy by her rivals; nowadays it is dissension between the United States and her chief associates which also hampers the free world. In the earlier period Britain was challenged by her enemies; more recently it is the partners of the United States who have likewise been restive. The enemies of the United States may toil to bring her low; it is the illusion of American omniscience which her own allies resent. Coalition diplomacy calls for teamwork but to elicit this from others the leader of the team must manifest it himself.

And for such a critique of American primacy there may since have been ample warrant. But, after the Truman Doctrine and Marshall Plan, the United States had perceived the earth-girdling nature of the global contest when, by signing the North Atlantic Alliance (4 April 1949), she rendered Western Europe much more secure. Without it the Russians, holding down East Germany, might have intimidated the Bonn Republic as the Americans, with others, were engaged so heavily elsewhere. North Korea, incited by Moscow and sustained by the Chinese allies of the Soviet Union, had to be stopped from overrunning South Korea, an American ward, and from thus enabling the East to establish itself across narrow waters from the postwar American occupation of Japan.

In 1956, on the other hand, Washington itself did a lot to erode its own global stakes when Messrs Eisenhower and Dulles facilitated a Soviet grip on the Middle East by their sabotage of the Anglo-French expedition against Egypt. After that initial Suez episode, with the North Atlantic Alliance almost split asunder, six West European countries, by signing the Treaty of Rome (25 March 1957), founded the European Community. And those were turning-points of which the United States has not heard the last. Spun out was to be her own unfinished business in the Middle East as well as in Western Europe.

Before this, nevertheless, the animosities of World War II had faded and the West Germans became more Atlantic-minded than the Gaullist French. During the 1950s, and long before outright American intervention in Vietnam, American diplomacy was brusque and overbearing but not without cause. Today the demands upon the United States, despite pockets of neo-isolationism, are still intercontinental – even if there have been changes of venue. Yet for the maintenance in common of a free world order, West European allies still do less than they might. And neither are arrears in that sphere likely to render Atlantic relationships more harmonious.

11 Western Europe versus the United States?*

Two renowned statesmen, John Kennedy and Charles de Gaulle, did most to symbolise a lingering difference in attitude towards the Atlantic nexus. The French President called for a European Europe – one devoid of American influence. The American President, on the contrary, advocated an Atlantic partnership that would bring the two sides of the North Atlantic more closely together.

The following analysis appeared in January 1963, soon after John Kennedy had settled the grave dispute with Nikita Krushchev of Russia over the installation of Soviet missiles in Cuba and just before Charles de Gaulle was to veto so resoundingly a British application for membership in the European Economic Community. Kennedy and de Gaulle were thus at their zenith when the divergence between them, despite subsequent variations in detail, became a problem for the West as a whole.

Europe and America are like a married couple who cannot live happily together yet cannot live apart. Their marriage, so far as it derives from mutual interest rather than a romantic attachment, might, in the old days, have been described as a marriage of convenience. A marriage of inconvenience would, however, be a more apt description of a union in which partners who are incompatible in many respects yet are welded indissolubly together. It is comforting that wedded bliss is not conspicuous in the Sino-Soviet household. There is solace in the fact, too, that when the West is challenged from with-

*This essay was first published as an article, 'A Marriage of Inconvenience', in *Foreign Affairs* (New York, Jan 1963). It constituted the final section of a symposium to which the other contributors were Dean Acheson, Christian A. Herter, Henry A. Kissinger and Malcom W. Hoag.

Some passages from that article were paraphrased by the writer in several chapters of a previous book. A number of these, with minor revisions in style, are, with others, here brought together again.

out, domestic friction diminishes. But it is not only against a chronic threat from the East that it has had to close ranks. There are new developments within the West, and as it tries to adjust itself to these it may be thrown into a vexatious disarray.

Two of the recent stages in the marriage of Europe and America are familiar enough: Europe spurned by America between the wars; America striving so bountifully after World War II to bring Europe back to life. But now another stage has been reached. Europe, having been restored, feels less dependent on America than before; separation if not divorce from its consort is in the air. Will the European independence that America itself fostered go too far? Further, is the new relationship more likely than the old to drag everybody into nuclear war? Independence at what price? That is, for both Europe and America, one of the great unanswered questions.

To check the disruptive and stress the cohesive – such is the task confronting the United States as leader of the West. President Kennedy, borrowing a theme from Eisenhower and Macmillan, therefore suggested a Declaration of Interdependence.

Declarations of that sort, with a short life expectancy, are supposed to signify a measure of accord between signatories. Rancour ensued when, during the 1970s, a new transatlantic one, the Ottawa Declaration, was drafted.

When, moreover, Kennedy remarked on July 4, 1962, that the United States will be ready to discuss with a united Europe the ways and means of forming a concrete Atlantic partnership, he also envisaged it as not only fortifying the defense of the free world but as looking outward to co-operate with all nations in meeting their common concerns. He did not add that an inward-looking Europe might aggravate rather than allay current perplexities. But it well might.

Defense may not be the sole realm in which the destiny of free nations is decided, but unless they prevail there, others will. Isolationists and appeasers yesterday, pacifists and neutralists today, have been reluctant to admit this basic truth;

but it is not by evading the realities of power that free societies can perpetuate themselves. In how good a position is Europe now to fend for itself? Will it be more able than it has been to set the terms for Atlantic interdependence? Peace-keeping in the postwar world has been mainly the duty of the United States. To what extent will a unified Europe be prepared to take this duty over?

How is peace kept? There would have been no major wars if the one over-riding aim of the Atlantic peoples had not been, at turning points in the twentieth century, the preservation of a free world order. In World War I that free world order could still best be preserved by maintaining the balance of power in Europe. But since Pearl Harbor, the area of wartime conflict has been enlarged, and since World War II so has the scope of peacetime competition. Peace has been maintained by a global balance of power underwritten for the West by the United States. Europe, while still a most crucial sector, is but one among others. During the nineteenth century the *Pax Britannica* profited from Britain's world-wide command of the seas and a favorable balance of power in Europe. Now in the second half of this century, however, Europeans have not been able to uphold by themselves the European segment of a global equilibrium. That is why a North American presence in NATO Europe has served as more than a symbol and supplement. What makes it so formidable is the fact that it is part of a global power structure of which the nuclear sea and air power of the United States is the world-wide prop.

That, moreover, is not the whole story. Although nobody in the nuclear missile age can win a major war with arms, the free world without arms would lose its freedom. Peace by power is thus still the watchword for the West. But as East and West deter each other in the military sphere, they vie all the harder with each other in the non-military sphere. Furthermore, the distribution of power between the rival camps has not merely brought forth an East-West equilibrium. Interior forces within each camp get from it a certain lattitude for asserting themselves. Where would be a unified Europe, where would be Adenauer or de Gaulle, without it? Where would be those in Britain who have equated

Soviet offensive missiles in Cuba with NATO missile bases? Where would be its Afro-Asian critics and detractors?

Neutralists might have been courted less assiduously if so much of the struggle between the antagonistic concepts of world order, the free one and the Communist one, had not shifted to the non-military sphere. As it is, some of the relatively powerless states acquire a chance to speak as though they possessed substantial power. And within the West itself a redistribution of power is rendered feasible by global power guarantees to which the United States still contributes most. Nor is the East untouched by change. Russia and China have been reshuffling their cards, and the manner in which they adapt themselves to each other must also impinge profoundly on the prospects of the West, just as will the manner in which Europe and America adapt themselves to any Atlantic redistribution of power.

The command of the deterrent is above all in dispute. Can Europe be embroiled without America or can America be embroiled without Europe? They cannot. Such immunity is ruled out by war plans; by modern war technology; by the world-wide range of the East-West contest itself; by a strategic interlock; by the fact that an adversary will regard the defense system of the West as a single mechanism and mount his assaults accordingly. Europe cannot remove itself from the line of fire simply by reconstructing its economy; to do that it would have to contract out of its alliance with America and submit to Moscow. The degree to which the allies of the United States were meshed with it in a strategic interlock was what worried them during the Korean War and subsequent events in the Far East. They asked whether those in charge of American policy might become trigger-happy. Now some Europeans nourish the opposite fear. They wonder whether the United States will expose herself to nuclear retaliation on their behalf.

Is it likely that in a European emergency the United States would do too little rather than too much? Britain did not wish to be caught short, and that was one of her motives when she built her own deterrent; but she did so in co-ordination with the United States. Though the French belong to the North Atlantic Alliance, they never joined

NATO, the organisation through which it works. Nor have they been getting the same sort of nuclear information as Britain for building their own deterrent. The United States may or may not withhold this nuclear information from them much longer. But the French themselves cannot tell what kind of a regime it will be to which they want American nuclear secrets, so vital for the defence of the West, entrusted. With their flair for invoking reason to mask unreason, they demand that the United States and Britain have more faith in them than they, before, during and since Vichy, have had in each other. In a unified Europe the French would have to share the direction of their nuclear deterrent with others. Yet it can be a vehicle not only for achieving equality for Western Europe but for ensuring their own semi-continental pre-eminence. The budgetary costs for France will, however, be astronomical. And, if Europeans beggar themselves to attain a full complement of nuclear arms, it might well be that they could not attain parity in other respects.

Europe and America are bound to argue over these differing estimates of future contingencies so long as the East-West contest lasts. In dispute is whether a unified Europe, regional in ambit, should have equal access to the levers of a global power apparatus that, among the nations of the West, only the United States has had the means to create and keep up. There may be no room on the trigger for more than one finger. What if there is more than one trigger?

There might, in fact, be more than one trigger if there is a European deterrent which is not coordinated with the over-all American deterrent. An alternative would be to assign the European deterrent to NATO where it could, perhaps, be run by Europeans and Americans together. If a NATO deterrent was so coordinated with the over-all American deterrent, the United States could still exercise ultimate control over the nuclear defense of the West. But if it was not so coordinated, how safe would be the West as a whole? It is of course possible that in time a unified Europe may discover how its demand for equality of status can be reconciled with its supreme need to avert any fateful mismanagement of the strategic interlock. That discovery is not in sight.

As for uncertainty about the American course, there should be less of this after the latest phase of the Cuban missile crisis. More uncertain are the influences to which, as a nuclear equal, a unified Europe might be subjected. The all-encompassing range of the East-West contest itself would, at any rate, compel the United States to act.

Western Europe has from the outset been the chief prize of that world contest. If the Communist East were to acquire sway over Western Europe – with its human resources, its physical plant, its central strategic position – the global balance of power would shift irretrievably against the United States. Europeans might recall that during World Wars I and II Europe was nearly lost before the United States came to the rescue. American leadership and the present global balance of power are not alone in having altered all that; the very nature of nuclear weapons themselves has altered it also. To be held, Europe must be held now.

Twice, in a phrase more prescient than Canning himself could appreciate, the New World has been called into existence to redress the balance of the Old. Now the New World has called the Old World into existence to redress a balance that extends to the limits of the earth. No reversal of roles could be operationally more significant, and it is in this light that Europeans must assess it.

Time has thus brought another of its strange revenges. Two antithetical theories impel the would-be architects of a unified Europe, and in both they may be ill-advised. They contend that, in the long run, they cannot count on the United States; conversely they are tempted to believe that, in the short run, whatever they do the United States is bound to back them up. But it is so bound and it isn't. A unified Europe would suffer if it drove the United States in upon herself. Europeans should remember that the American political system is not geared for the kind of leadership that the United States has of necessity had to exercise since the last war, and that there are elements in it which would be glad to take advantage of opportunities to diminish the burdens of that leadership. The United States, to be sure, might have done even better. It is a miracle that, with key elements in the Congress hankering for a protectionist and isolationist past, it has done so well.

Meanwhile, in any attempt to form a concrete Atlantic partnership attention will be centered on its economic rather than its strategic features. When the Common Market comes to negotiate lower tariffs with the Kennedy Administration it will boggle at the 'Buy American' act; escape clauses will not escape attention; Europe will ask that discriminatory taxation and unfair customs practices be abolished. But in return Washington can remind Europeans that a disproportionate American expenditure on foreign aid and overseas defense has heavily contributed to a balance-of-payments deficit and the drastic outflow of gold. And now, after further Russian triumphs in space, the United States may feel it must spend more on the race to the moon. Can the United States whittle down its military expenditures in Europe and its aid to the underdeveloped countries without asking that a bigger share be shouldered by flourishing European beneficiaries? If they insist upon equality of status, NATO costs might be a test case. Equal is as equal does.

On both sides of the Atlantic the broadest perspectives will be required. Washington has often been highhanded, but Europeans must remember that American blunders do not erase from the record those greater European misjudgments that brought the United States, at once so brash and so reluctant, to the fore. Have American booms not been permanent? Far from eternal is the European boom. A recent American setback may tempt Europeans, not without a hint of malicious glee, to cut their own American benefactor down to size; but, unless the European stake in American prosperity has evaporated, any such vindictiveness would be self-frustrating. Jeshurun having waxed fat may kick, but care must be taken lest he also injure himself. The way in which the United States exercises the leadership of the West may not always be predictable. But as Americans try to imagine what a unified Europe will be like and how it will behave in the mooted Atlantic partnership they encounter many unknowns also.

It may be a more highly integrated Europe than most Europeans themselves yet realize. Resting upon a customs union and an economic union, the new European edifice is to be rounded out by a political union. And that is not surprising, since the modern politico-economy is not separated into watertight compartments. What happens where barriers still constrict? Quite pragmatically, and without resort to doctrine, the state's powers to integrate may come into play. If state powers are needed to get things done across the length and breadth of Western Europe, then a larger statehood may, under one label or another, swallow up component states.

And this is why European federalists can wait with comparative serenity for President de Gaulle to vanish from the scene. A union of states such as he has proposed may not long withstand the pressure for closer integration that a unified Europe must generate of its own accord. The adoption of supranational powers might be delayed by squabbles like those between French and West German agriculture. To overcome these it could also be speeded up.

An American prototype has shown the shape of things to come. But trade is not the only sphere in which the example set by the United States may prefigure the future of Europe. The Common Market does what the United States did when it organized a customs union in a semi-continental expanse; when, removing tariffs among insiders, it made then uniform against outsiders. By the same token, however, a unified Europe might have to do what the United States did in all other branches of the American economy. Among free societies it is the most successful pioneer of bigness. So with the Common Market – the greater the flow of European trade, the tighter the grip of bigness on the European economy. But it cannot tighten its grip on the European economy without deepening the general pattern of European integration.

Trade and bigness interact, and when they do so the ground is cleared for that federal merger through which alone the full potentialities of the entire venture can best be fulfilled. The paths taken may be diverse, uneven, circuitous, without the usual signposts; the European Communities might provide novel modalities. It may be that within a political union there could be no outright pooling of sovereignty without the consent of members. What members themselves cannot do is delimit the energies which a customs union will have released and which an economic union will have quickened on an ever-enlarging scale. Deep-seated particularisms in language and culture might still impede, but even if these are not swept away they may be bypassed as a unified Europe consolidates itself indivisibly.

None of this will be feasible, however, when inflation is rampant and a hurly-burly over the price of oil may always make it worse. Politics, besides, cannot be pursued as the shortest distance between two points; nor does the foregoing analysis, it might be fair to add, refer to the calendar. A European Union by 1980, as agreed at a Community summit by Messrs Pompidou, Heath and Brandt, was an objective absurdly premature; it would be foolish of Messrs Giscard d'Estaing and Helmut Schmidt to reaffirm it. Yet only some in Britain are on the alert against those routine decrees from Brussels which override Parliament and are thus, in themselves, a unifying Community procedure.

As long as the European Community hopes to act in world affairs as a single unit, it may swerve from side to side or even retrace its steps without letting itself break up. Reculer pour mieux sauter, *even if subconscious, may yet derive from a basic common impulse. When, too, various components thus cling together, an innate drive towards organic union may some day resume. And what must then be asked is not how tautly it is bound but how large, if the power structure of the West is to stay intact, the European Community should be.*

The United States has given its blessing to the closest integration of Europe, economic and political. But would it be pleased if, as the many are replaced by one, particularism is not banished? If, as applied to defense, diplomacy, world trade and international finance, European particularism is merely projected on a larger screen? The irony of that for the United States would be evident.

It is expected that a unified Europe will have the ability to say 'no' in unison to the United States as well as 'yes'. The desired unison may be achieved on an American model. In other words, the more American techniques are assimilated, the more capable Europeans will be of resisting American counsels. Today it may not only have been postwar subsidies from the United States that will have helped a unified Europe, if it so wishes, to diverge from America. The processes by which America itself was, as it were, Americanized will also help.

This paradox should be understood. The United States could never have Americanized others by its own unaided efforts. But when others emulate America in the American style of life, based as it is on mass production coupled with a free movement of trade, people and classes in a semi-continental area, they may Americanize themselves. A unified Europe will give bigness a greater chance in a region that historically has prided itself on its rejection of bigness. And self-Americanization might enable a Third Force, under the nuclear protective shield of the United States, to go it alone.

Let us now look at the political auguries if the unification of Western Europe moves ahead. Whatever serves to bury the hatchet between French and Germans deserves the thanks of mankind. But the underlying goals of the two peoples are not the same. France is a satisfied power, while the Bonn Republic, like Germany between the wars, is a dissatisfied one. From Bismarck to Hitler, the two Germanys, now sundered from each other, were a single state for less than 75 years; and for their partition between East and West the German people have only themselves to blame. Yet, so as to keep the Bonn Republic well disposed toward the West, the West has had to champion its claims for German reunification. This objective could be achieved only on terms that would undo the pending unification of Western Europe and conflict, in the global equilibrium, with the West's own defense of its European sector.

For what, then, is Moscow waiting? A neutral Reich, in which the Soviets had permitted a satellite to rejoin the Bonn Republic, could deny the West strategic access to German soil and deprive it of economic access to the heavy industries of the Ruhr. But it could also mean that Russia would again have to cope with a greater Germany; and among Russians as well as in the captive states of Eastern Europe the memory of German invasions is still fresh. After Moscow's experience with its Chinese ally it may prefer to have fewer and not more major powers seated on the rim of the Russian imperium. Nor can the Soviet realm be integrated economically if it relinquishes East German resources.

Ever since the turn of the century there has been interaction between European and East Asian affairs. Moscow again had to cope with a Eurasian defense shuttle when, after the defeat of Japan, it kept an eye fixed on China. And as long as Russia must also watch Asian frontiers, Germany will be left comparatively weak. A reunion of a German client State with the Bonn Republic is, accordingly, sure to be excluded.

All this Bonn has conceded to Moscow for the time being under Ostpolitik. *The question can be reopened, however, if enmity between Russia and China should prove less than eternal.*

Ostpolitik *enables the Soviet Union to maintain the* status quo *on two fronts about which traditionally it has had to think first of all – but when, in addition, a missile onslaught by sea and air from two other fronts is now also possible. For that is what a global contest may offer when Russia still tries, by her own self-centred concept of peaceful co-existence, to promote the undoing of the* status quo *elsewhere.*

There are two problems here, that of fitting Western Germany into a unified Europe and that of fitting a unified Europe into a more concrete Atlantic partnership. These two problems cannot be treated apart. It may be noted that defeat and occupation by Germans seem to have left less of a scar on official France than the ill will exhibited by her American ally – a recent liberator – during the Suez crisis. A deterrent of their own might now embolden the French to talk back openly to Washington. But a global balance is what made them secure as they extricated themselves from Indochina and North Africa, staged their sit-down strike against NATO and let the Fourth Republic be overthrown. Nor has the American guarantee, with or without a European deterrent, outlived its usefulness.

The French have resented Anglo-American solidarity and have wanted to combine with the United States and Britain in a sort of three-power directorate for the West. But what confidence can they have inspired in Washington and London? Who, when the Gaullist regime comes to an end, will speak for France – the Army, the extreme Right, the extreme Left?

The Chancellor of the Bonn Republic, Herr Willy Brandt, had just resigned because a Communist assistant could pilfer defense papers when, only by a hair's breadth, the French people voted, in May 1974, against a Presidential candidate whose tenure of office would have had, as its sturdiest crutch, a highly disciplined Communist Party.

M. Mitterand might not have assigned sensitive portfolios to Communist members of his Cabinets. Among such colleagues, all the same, there is much to be picked up whatever precautions are taken. Soon, as Communist ministers acquired respect, they would be privy to communications with the North Atlantic Alliance, of which, by hook or crook, Moscow might rapidly be apprised. And what also should have been a shock to the West was that virtually half of the French people did not seem to care.

President de Gaulle may dream his dream of a tranquil Europe stretching from the Atlantic to the Urals. But since this entails a basic shift in power alignments it implies that a European Third Force, over which the French will preside, can make its own settlement with the Soviet Union. But *sauve qui peut* was a Napoleonic cry that the French, above all, should remember; before a Third Force deserts the United States the United States might desert it. A bilateral settlement with Washington is what Moscow, cognizant of global power realities, has long sought. Western Europe should be the last to push the United States into that kind of a settlement.

It is under these circumstances that the United States, torn between hopes and fears, has urged that some room be found for Britain in the new unified Europe. If this were done it would not only ensure a more outward-looking attitude by the Common Market toward questions of trade and economic policy; it also would reduce the element of political risk. The Belgians, the Dutch, the Luxembourgers, the Italians (together with Britain's own cosignatories of the European Free Trade Association) have been apprehensive over the prospect of West German, French or Franco-German predominance. A British counterweight might avert that danger. A European Third Force, moreover, would be at variance with American leadership of the West, and here again Britain could do the most to stabilize. Britain, however, is not as strong as she was and she could not act as a European stabilizer if, as a component of a European federal merger, she were cut off from overseas sources of strength. One of these overseas sources of strength is the Commonwealth. Anglo-American friendship is another. And indeed they have long been interconnected.

On strategic issues, *e.g.* regarding the disposition of the deterrent, it is imperative that Britain and the United States should keep in step. For the time may soon come when, as a nuclear power, Britain will wish to chart a new course. Will it be safe if she amalgamates the British segment of the Western deterrent with that of France? How could Britain belong to a European political union and not do so? What view will Washington take?

Washington will feel less anxiety if a unified Europe does not cling to the command of any joint deterrent of its own but assigns it to NATO. For, through such an arrangement, the United States might still have the last word. But what if other deterrents in the West are not assigned to NATO? Then, if the British segment of the over-all deterrent must be transferred anywhere, it should be, surely, to the United States. For in every aspect of policy, and not just in one as momentous as this, Anglo-American friendship remains, acknowledged or unacknowledged, the mainstay of the West.

To restate that truth today may be to run against the tide. It nevertheless must be restated, and on both sides of the Atlantic. A free world order might never have survived if, at the gravest junctures in the twentieth century, the Anglo-American link had not pre-existed. Since World War II it has had – from the Far East to the Congo and Cuba – its characteristic ups and downs. But so rooted is Anglo-American friendship in the national interests of Britain and the United States that even the tragic Anglo-American divergence over Suez could not destroy it.

And now it is because the United States relies on Britain that she wants Britain to play a part in the unification of Europe. In the American approach to Europe it is not only assumed that the United States will persist as leader of the West but that, as she does so, Britain will march with her. It will be asked whether most of the British people still want to march with the United States. Two recent B.B.C. talks, published in *The Listener,* depicted Anglo-American friendship as an unhistorical myth.* But then truth is always a myth for those who have myths of their own to purvey.

As Europe and America re-group, what will be the British role? Opponents and proponents of her entry into the Common Market have both often taken it for granted that what confronts Britain is a choice between Europe and the Commonwealth. That, however, is a false antithesis. The real issue is Britain's status. If Britain retains an independent status, the Commonwealth fellowship, despite any quarrel over trade agreements, may still go on; if Britain cannot retain an independent status – if she is converted into a mere outer island province of a European Union – the Commonwealth will dissolve automatically, and so will an Anglo-American factor that has been another overseas source of British strength. Britain in the twentieth century has been like a tripod with a leg for Europe, a leg for the fellowship of the Commonwealth, a leg for ties with the United States. Conditions may alter. It is on the three legs of its tripod, and not on any one or two, that Britain must still stand.

It will be complex to make that unified Europe which, as the United States has conceived it, would be one of two equal pillars in the Atlantic edifice. The nature of the pillar on the American side of the Atlantic has never been described. Is Canada, for instance, to be included? The European pillar is to be cemented by close integration. But Canada, seeking to keep a national identity of her own, has long resisted close intergration with her southern neighbour.

It is a question, too, where the Latin American countries will fit in, since in a hemispherically unified America they might be liabilities rather than assets. Europe as well as America must do what it can for Latin America. But Latin America has little with which to reciprocate, and it is only on a basis of reciprocity that a concrete Atlantic partnership, as advocated by President Kennedy, can function.

*5 Oct 1961 and 23 Aug 1962. The *Listener* (London 20 Sep 1962) watered down a letter of protest.

Two points arise, one negative and one positive. The accent is on the negative when Europe and America do not pull together. But fortunately their rivals in the East labor under even greater disabilities. Russia and China are assuredly no mere laths painted to look like iron; but Communist economies will have to do better if they are to go on mesmerising some of the neutralist nations. Moreover, though Europe and America might differ over the common defense, the two main sections of the Sino-Soviet camp may yet have to defend themselves against each other. Thus where the West cannot by its own exertions save itself, the East, by its dissensions, may help save the West.

The West will stultify itself if its frame of reference is too narrow – if European issues are not put in an Atlantic setting and if Atlantic issues are not put in a setting that, as with the Commonwealth and Anglo-American friendship, is actually world-wide. Peoples that are underprivileged or newly emancipated may be confused as they make their bow on the world stage; for Europeans and Americans there is less excuse. As long as they uphold freedom and order on a world-wide basis the values of civilised society will be sustained. In upholding them Europe and America may forge new unities. Old-established ones must, at the same time, also be preserved.

12 The American Role and World Order*

The Korean War was fought in the name of the United Nations and the chief allies of the United States sent token forces. When the United States intervened at the side of South Vietnam some were dispatched again by countries with regional interests but others refrained. Such abstention by her allies in the West irked official Washington. It had, though, no adverse fallout among the American people as a whole. Soul-searching over what the United States was doing in Southeast Asia had become too intense.

Few in the West could be indifferent to the plight of Vietnam and the turmoil American participation was fomenting on the home front. During the Korean War there had been alarm over abuses of authority by General Douglas MacArthur and Senator Joseph McCarthy. War in Vietnam evoked on both sides of the Atlantic something even more serious – an overall disenchantment with American leadership by which civilised society itself could be imperilled. It was to this solemn topic that in 1967 the following essay addressed itself.

'It is not the purpose of the United States to impose a *Pax Americana* around the world,' Mr Dean Rusk has declared. 'We don't consider ourselves the gendarmes of the universe.' American intentions are, nevertheless, still suspect, and this disclaimer was rejected at once by the Washington correspondent of *The Times* (London). 'There is agreement that Britain should remain east of Suez,' he reported from Washington to London, 'if only because the United States seems anxious for company in its self-appointed role as global gendarme.'

*This essay was first published as an article in the *Yale Review* (New Haven, Conn., Jun 1967). One outdated paragraph, with other superfluous material, has been discarded.

As a critique of that role no dictum could be more succinct. For its cogency, however, there is less to be said.

Even if free countries wished to reject American leadership in theory they could not do so in practice; the United States herself cannot throw it off. For the American role is shaped by the nature of the world in which we live. And the nature of that world is ignored when there is talk about the American role as that of a self-appointed global gendarme.

Such a gibe appears to suggest that no custodian of world order is needed. It also appears to suggest that if a custodian is needed there is machinery by which he can be appointed, by which a mandate as global gendarme can be assigned more legitimately. But what it tends to suggest, above all, is that the militancy of others has not been the danger in our time. Caprice in leadership by the United States – that, presumably, is the source of trouble.

Credence may be given to this portrait of America as a self-appointed gendarme by those among the British who recollect the termination of Lend-Lease, and Suez and Skybolt. No nation, all the same, has more reason to adduce other evidence to the contrary and, by its own national experience, put the American role in perspective. For, under altered conditions, the United States, as leader of the West, has only been taking a leaf out of the British book. Britain's own role, after all, was a 'self-appointed' one when free countries (including the United States) developed overseas under the shelter of British sea power; when ideas of freedom took root among people not yet free; when, too, Britain stood alone between civilized society and its debasement by the Nazis. It is odd that in this day and age such truths have to be restated. They would not have to be restated if, at the heart of the West, a woeful incomprehension of the forces in play did not exist.

It is only a quarter of a century since a second German sweep across Europe, the Battle of Britain, and the Japanese assault at Pearl Harbor blew sky-high the inward-looking concept of Fortress America. Is the pendulum going to swing back? As American roles, that of Fortress America and that of the United States as world policeman, would be diametrically opposed. The first was never a tenable one. The United

States has never adopted the second. But why should the Secretary of State have to deny that she has?

None of this would matter if the charge Mr Rusk has had to meet came solely from the foes of America and the West. Their animus is a gauge of what they have been up against. But for some years a number of sober-minded Americans have wondered whether, in the world arena, American initiatives were really paying off. They were shocked by American landings in the Dominican Republic and now the war in Vietnam is scarcely calculated to cheer them up. Yet illusion was no safe guide between the wars. Disillusion, by the same token, will be no safe guide today.

What, then, has the United States been doing? Before an attempt is made to answer that question another question must be tackled. For critics, American and non-American, do not always make clear whether they are finding fault with American policy as manifested in specific areas and episodes or whether their quarrel is with the total American role. American policy in specific areas or episodes may be one way of implementing the American role; it may not be the only way. Critics of American policy have an indispensable service to render; it is an imperative of democracy that their function be cherished. But they, too, may have to think again when a total revision in the pattern of American leadership is what their doubts would entail. It may be hard to draw a line between critiques of various American policies and critiques of the basic American role. That line must, nevertheless, be drawn.

All this raises yet another question – one that is absolutely fundamental. What, some critics must be asked, would the world be like if the United States did not play her great part? Between the wars there was a school of American progressives that tended to espouse one philosophy for domestic politics and another for international affairs. A hangover from the parish-pump mentality of pioneer days, it could not outlast Pearl Harbor. Those who have labored for social and racial justice at home have envisaged no narrow limits for intervention by the State. There can, similarly, be no narrow limits for American intervention abroad if liberal values are to be preserved across the seas, if a free world order is to be perpetuated.

It is in the light of the past that first things must still be put first. Those who erected the postwar defenses of the West did so with prewar errors in mind. Not all isolationists on one side of the Atlantic, nor all appeasers on the other, were fools, knaves, or cynics. Many simply mistook escapism for idealism. Misjudgment on the Right, it should be recalled, had often begun on the Left. And yet even for idealists there is no escape from the realities of power. Those for example, who now look forward to an overriding authority vested in the United Nations perceive that peace must be enforced. They do not assume, as some do assume, that the security enjoyed by the free world is automatic. And if there is nothing automatic about peace, the leadership which the United States provides is no curse but a blessing.

Here, then, is the central issue. But after the passage of the years many of the younger generation may not get it straight. Nor can all neutralists be expected to grasp it with ease. Their countries have been preoccupied with the struggle for independence; and yet only as the West prevails is that independence worth much. But nearer home there are also some who regard free rides as their due. They might indict the manner in which the United States exerts her power. If that power lay slack and unexerted, they themselves would be lost.

Such were lessons taught by two German bids for hegemony. During the Second World War the West saw at last that, as world politics are a contest for power, its own power for peace must be brought to bear unremittingly. Under American leadership the West has staved off a third bid for hegemony. One that might stem from her Chinese neighbor is what now worries Russia herself. Critics of American policy, American and non-American, may take for granted much that the United States has accomplished. It is by what the United States has accomplished that antagonists are embittered.

And no turning point in this respect could be more significant than the Russo-American crisis of October 1962. Fresh detail may be rounding out the story of how President Kennedy persuaded Chairman Khrushchev to withdraw Soviet missiles from Cuba. Though this stroke was epoch-making, its full import is still often misunderstood even by European admirers of President Kennedy. For Soviet missiles, by their presence in Cuba, could have been employed to curb American action, and American action could not be curbed without many regions beyond North America also being subjected to Russian blackmail. The fate of Eastern Europe indicated what was in store for Western Europe if, after the Second World War, the United States had reverted voluntarily to hemispheric isolationism. An involuntary American isolationism, with all its dire consequences for the rest of the free world, was what the Kremlin tried to extort in the autumn of 1962. The West, under American leadership, could not be outflanked. Russia thereupon was compelled to take another course. By 1966, when Mr Kosygin mediated between India and Pakistan at Tashkent, caution rather than audacity had become Russia's own motivating force.

It was, to be sure, on Peking rather than Washington that Moscow had its eye. Russia could not allow China to fish in troubled waters below the Himalayas; any Chinese quest for the mastery of East Asia had to be forestalled. But it is the vigil maintained by the United States and her allies which makes it more difficult for Russia to cope with the hostility of China. Foes on more than one front constitute a risk that the Russians, like the Germans, will not soon welcome again. And if the Chinese threat should induce a change of heart in Moscow towards the West, Washington may owe more to Peking than it will admit.

Other problems enter into the reckoning. Nuclear proliferation is a universal menace and Russia must have an accord against this as much as any nation. Nor can Russian consumer wants be neglected. Then, too, punches are likely to be pulled when the agricultural segment of Communist economies is so primitive. And when these economies must purchase wheat from North America, Washington (together with Ottawa and Canberra) has another element to add to its power for peace.

Moscow will bow to this power with the utmost reluctance. Russia has not been a conciliator at Hanoi as she has been at Tashkent because North Vietnam is a focus of her own two feuds – not only of that with China but also of that with the West which, though now a less deep-seated one, is still unsettled. Strange is the peacemaker who fosters the idea of war – those 'wars of liberation' which do not liberate. For under peaceful coexistence, as Moscow proclaims it, the means have changed but not the end. And yet, if the means change, the end, under steady American strategic pressure, might change as well.

Within the next decade such optimism became less rather than more tenable. Russia had overtaken the United States in the air, at sea and on land. Enrichissez vous! *was, besides, old Guizot's advice, and with the exception of Britain West Europeans have lately been enriching themselves – before, that is, inflation made its ravages felt. It never failed to irritate Washington, during these years, that they could afford to spend more on the common defense but did not.*

A settlement between Russia and the West is not around the corner. But Russia is being left with no alternative. And by that fact, too, the American role may be vindicated.

One difference between its adversaries and its critics should, at any rate, be singled out. Adversaries dare not ignore power realities. Critics, on the other hand, can do so precisely because the United States, taking the rough with the smooth, has handled power realities with overall success. There may, nevertheless, be a genuine misunderstanding when American efforts to reinforce a free world order are accused of being overdone–when the American role is decried as an attempt to police the world. For the United States, after being sheltered by British power during her own years of growth, has taken Britain's place at a juncture when the dimensions of leadership have become more vast. And vast is the strain under which this puts any leader of the West. One reason why Americans and the friends of America are confused about the American role is the sheer magnitude of those dimensions.

The United States is not the first to do what she is doing. When a free world order depended on Britain, the scale of things was also world-wide. But then, while the instruments of primacy were the Royal Navy and an Empire on which the sun never set, it was only in Europe that Britain had to have a favorable balance of power. Now the scope of world contests has been greatly enlarged in extent and depth – quite apart from the tremendous range of desolating new weapons. Europeans themselves demolished the old European balance of power in the two major wars of the twentieth century. It has been supplanted by a global balance. And this is a state of affairs into which the United States herself was catapulted. She did not invent it. If others are governed by it, so is she.

But the United States cannot allow it to be exploited against her or against those with whom she is closely linked. No heavy adverse shift in the global balance would therefore be safe. When Britain maintained or restored the old European balance of power, she also protected the weak against the strong. On distant sectors of a larger world balance, however, only a more selective approach can be undertaken. Never have the strategic risks been so grave while, despite huge strides forward in air transport, geography still impedes. Nor has the United States earned plaudits when she has helped some of the weak fend off the clutches of the strong. It will take more than the rhetoric of Gaullism to resurrect the traditional European balance of power. But now even Russia, against whom the European sector of the global balance has had to be upheld, must want the East Asian sector of the global balance maintained against the Communist Chinese.

The West, under American leadership, has kept Western Europe out of hostile hands. There is less to work with in Eastern Asia and it may be impracticable, politically and logistically, to pull off a repeat performance on all Asian sectors of the global balance. Yet ever since the turn of the century the plight of East Asia has been an item on the American agenda. Quite literally the United States was a 'paper tiger' when, from John Hay to Henry Stimson, she imagined she could have the Open Door and territorial integrity of China preserved without the comforts of isolationism being abandoned.

Theodore Roosevelt won fame when, giving his assent in secret to a renewal of the Anglo-Japanese Alliance, he mediated in the Russo-Japanese War. His goal was an equilibrium between Russia and Japan that, as war crises started to interact between Europe and the Far East, would gratuitously preserve the American position in the Pacific. It could not be preserved gratuitously.* Now it is China herself that most of her neighbors fear. Some of them have banded together against her. And the time may come when a more solid regional equilibrium will emerge. But until it does the United States, as the main guarantor of the global balance, cannot let its Asian sector be jeopardized unduly.

Even so, critics may argue, the locale of Vietnam was not a crucial one. The circumstances, it is true, have not been the same as they were in Korea. But while Vietnam has suffered, the rest of Asia may actually be better off. All that the United States has done might have caused the Communist Chinese to hesitate when they renewed pressure on India during the Indo-Pakistani hostilities of 1965. It could also have emboldened Indonesian generals (with Indonesia blocked anyway by British forces in Malaysia) to turn against President Sukarno, and thus rob China of a key adjunct for the conquest of Southeastern and Southern Asia, as well as a stepping stone toward Australasia. Many frown upon American intervention in Vietnam. Yet by-products as important as these, when a global balance has to be upheld, tend to redress a balance that is not merely strategic.

A specific American intervention must, at any rate, be assessed in a wider context. Those who scoff at the role of the United States as a global gendarme must take care lest they wind up condemning the necessity of American intervention in principle anywhere. An axiom less familiar today

*A new pattern in world politics was being hammered out, and the configuration of diplomacy before World War I had begun to take shape.

As a counterbalance to the Triple Alliance of the German Empire, the Austro-Hungarian Empire and the Kingdom of Italy, there was the Anglo-Japanese Alliance, the Anglo-French Entente and an Anglo-American factor. Mediating between Tsarist Russia and Imperial Japan, the President of the United States steered clear of a German challenge to the Entente Cordiale over Morocco – one that, by welding Britain and France together, was, with the inclusion of Tsarist Russia, soon transformed into the Triple Entente. Lionel Gelber, *The Rise of Anglo-American Friendship* (Oxford University Press, London and New York, 1938) pp. 167-275. Reissued by Archon Books, Hamden, Conn., 1966.

than it should be must therefore be reemphasized. When the United States does not intervene on some vulnerable sectors of the global balance, the road will be left open for interventions of quite another character. And to the validity of that axiom the entire history of the twentieth century bears grim witness. The West never recovered from the moral and political havoc of the First World War. It is too soon for the lessons of the Second World War to be spurned.

Ironies abound. The stigma of imperialism is attached to countervailing measures taken by the United States against the imperial expansion, overt or covert, of self-styled anti-imperialists. But then the United States herself once employed the language of anti-imperialism when, within the Western Hemisphere and in the acquisition of overseas outposts, American imperialism itself made its mark. An apparatus of overseas power underpinned a free world order in Britain's heyday. Perhaps the United States must have a similar apparatus unless a similar magic can be worked through mirrors.

There is neither a world policeman nor a world constabulary. It is only an approximation to a rule of law (one honored more often in the breach than the observance) that can somehow be enforced. And but for American preponderance, even that minimal enforcement could scarcely have been devised. The United States does not, however, act alone, and an ally like Britain does not act with her because, as a British critic avers, the United States is 'anxious for company'. Allies would not be allies if they were not equally anxious to have the company of the United States. A profound mutuality is the key to it all. The United States is head of a world-wide coalition because there is a free world order in which allies possess with the United States a commensurate stake.

The American role is no paradox and yet paradox is what dogs it. Honest critics, American and non-American, might, for example, be correct if they could still evaluate the American role by criteria that belong to a traditional frame of reference. But they cannot. Only a global frame of reference will now suffice. And, just as the dimensions of the power contest are much wider, so has ideology become a tool of power with a reach vaster than the reach of power itself.

Free institutions make the very task of upholding freedom more complex. Dictatorships like those of Communist China, North Vietnam, and the Soviet Union do not have to answer at home for what they do abroad. But American protests against American intervention in Vietnam might have suggested that the United States was about to falter in her resolve. And if this impression made Hanoi and Peking persist, it could have lengthened American casualty lists while the agony of the two Vietnams was prolonged. Representative democracy is the one type of political system that is morally sound. A moral boomerang could, nevertheless, thus spring from it.

Among the virtues of representative democracy, this is an innate defect. It can be coped with. In a representative democracy all must be free to speak out. But for it to be morally sound, it must also hold to account those who do speak out or who endeavour to serve it. Do critics, American and non-American, misconceive the very nature of modern power contests? Then dissent spoils its own case. The United States has had to proceed by trial and error. It is right when her errors are exposed. To expose the errors of those who sit in judgment is no less right. Do critics differentiate between critiques of American policy in particular and of the American role in general? For to be remiss in that respect is to befog and not clarify or enlighten.

Is it the contention of critics that, as global gendarme, the United States has been pushing others around more than she should? It is, as a matter of fact, inexcusable for critics, American and non-American, to talk of American 'domination' in the same breath as one talks of domination by Germans, Russians, and Chinese. For it is as a saving counterweight to their sort of power that American power has been thrown, tardily but fully, into the scales at last. 'Domination' is a term that, by any comparative standard, should not be misused. To apply it to the United States in the sense in which it must be applied to the tyrants and tormentors of the twentieth century is to debase the currency of political exchange. But while that kind of domination is a myth, as far as the United States is concerned, her predominance, though ineluctable, is something else again. And this predominance has not always been easy for others to take.

American predominance might rub allies and friends the wrong way less than it does if, over the years, the United States had been able to produce a political elite. Her social ethos and economic origins have militated against one. Despite the mistreatment of Negroes, the egalitarian tradition in American life runs deep. When the British were predominant they did not bother to please others. The British governing class could, nevertheless, renew itself as long as there was much to govern, and that fact, in itself, lent prestige. Even American public men like John Foster Dulles have been more Palmerstonian in essence than manner. Allies want the United States to redress disparities of power in the sphere of defense. But in other spheres, friends and neutrals might get on better with the United States if the background of American statesmen and officials were not as egalitarian as it is. In an egalitarian age the United States should have reaped substantial credit from the egalitarian spirit of American culture. This has not occurred.

In any survey of the American role there is a still more important paradox. Even allies who rely on the strategic predominance of the United States recoil from American economic 'domination'. The United States underwrites the security of the free world, and the unparalleled prosperity of the West is geared to hers. But her own beneficiaries must ward off the overflow of American productivity in export markets. And bound up with the superior competitive capacity of the United States is a massive investment potential through which the economy of others might be subjected more and more to American economic control. Not that there is a plot by the American corporate Establishment to deprive Canada of her national independence or to stir up undue resentment in Britain and the Common Market against any penetration that is economically inordinate. But no advanced country wants its chief resources or main industries to pass beyond its own control. And it is not in the American interest that they should. For robust, high-spirited allies rather than helpless economic satellites are what the United States needs to sustain her own world role.

The problem is without precedent. As long as there are threats to the West the allies of the United States cannot cut themselves off, politically and economically, from their own

American guarantor. And a new threat to the free world could arise if, by trying to disentangle themselves from her, they themselves shook the economic foundations of postwar prosperity and the entire political structure of the West. What the solution will be only time can tell. To withstand the American economic impact and yet make the most of the economic dynamism that the American economy generates – that is the predicament in which, by accident rather than design, a vibrant American titan has caught its own allies. The economic power and political energy of the United States are opposite sides of the same coin. She cannot have the one without the other. But neither can those to whom, like it or not, the American role means so much.

Lest she be overwhelmed, Canada has looked for offsets to the Commonwealth and the European Community. Among other industrialised countries, however, there is now more disquiet over the quadrupled price of oil and what Arab vandals may do with the proceeds. Not that the situation is similar to Le Defi Americain.* *As compared with the diverse foundations of the American economy abroad the Arab oil States have only a surfeit of fuel as a treasure trove on which to concentrate and for a period that may yet be short.*

One further point should be made. Not everything that mars the American image is to the discredit of the United States. A free semi-continental entity cannot be as consistent as nations that are less dispersed sectionally. More and more even Russia, with all its regimentation, has had to veer and tack in foreign affairs. Critics of the American role aver, however, that the American power system makes a drive toward 'world domination' inevitable. A 'wave of the future' is thus again being predicted; and fashionable pundits would presumably rewrite history, as did others in the era of the Nazi juggernaut, before it has occurred. But against them history itself can furnish an irrefutable corrective.

What can we learn from history about the American role? Surely that throughout the twentieth century the English-speaking peoples have not pursued world domination but

*This was the title of a widely-read book by Jean-Jacques Servan-Schreiber (Denöel, Paris, 1967).

mustered their power, sooner or later, to resist those who did. It may be that on occasion they have misused their power or espoused unwise policies. By and large, nevertheless, civilized society has been set back in the twentieth century because, until final crises, the free world has been not too assertive but too inert. American initiatives are not what should be viewed with alarm, but any sign that the United States might lose heart and retrench.

The United States as a 'self-appointed global gendarme' is, moreover, a theme with variations. President de Gaulle, for instance, has equated American and Russian power as that of two rival hegemonies from whose deadly opposition the rest of Europe should extricate itself. Gallic and Gaullist logic is, all the same, less than logical when he envisages a Third Force Europe that could mediate between these two colossi but yet would have an American guarantee to bolster it up. Tension between Russia and the United States, on the other hand, is not what enrages the Communist Chinese. A joint 'domination' by American and Russian colossi is the specter that haunts them – an encirclement that would check world domination by China herself.

Two world policemen would, no doubt, be better than a world without police. But they would not serve alone. Some of their allies will carry more weight than others. And it is rational that they should. More perilous than a combined domination is the inability of many, vociferate though they might, to follow through.

If the United States, together with Britain, had played a less pusillanimous part between the wars, mankind might have been spared not only its second long travail but that dread sequel, the East-West contest, by which it is still afflicted. The American people should not be discouraged from playing their great part now.

PART FIVE

The Atlantic Nexus Beyond the Atlantic

13 The United States, Britain and the Open Seas*

The West is a set of countries with concepts of freedom that extend far beyond an instrument of policy like the North Atlantic Alliance. The former, however, could not survive without the latter. The disparity between them resembles one to which the French refer when they distinguish between the pays réal *and the* pays légal. *It will be extraordinary, too, if, as has often been proposed, more is done to expand the existing coverage of the North Atlantic Alliance; most signatories fail to carry out current assignments as much as is urgently needed. One point raised by the next three chapters, all written and published during the 1970s, is how the West now has challenges to face beyond the specific boundaries of the North Atlantic Alliance. Never was the notion that Western Europe and North America can retire into their own shells more far-fetched or teamwork between them more essential.*

The free world has been slow to detect how, as Russia adopts policies of détente on the European continent and may even curb the apocalyptic race in nuclear weapons on land, she is not only girding her loins against Communist China but might also be clearing the decks for global supremacy through the element of sea-power. History can put this old-new challenge in perspective. The United States, after being sheltered by British naval power during her own years of growth, donned the mantle of leadership at a time when the dimensions of world contests have become vaster than ever before. Not that previous contests could be waged

*This essay comprises four-fifths of an article, 'Britain, Russia and the Open Seas', published in the *Spectator* (London, 31 Oct 1970).

There was a similar contribution by the present writer to *Commonwealth Policy In a Global Context,* ed. Paul Streeten and Hugh Corbet (Frank Cass & Co. Ltd, London, 1971) pp. 42-59.

within narrow confines. When a free world order relied on Britain the scale of things was also worldwide. But in that era, with instruments of primacy like the Royal Navy and an Empire on which the sun never set, it was only in Europe that Britain also had to have an adequate balance of power. An adequate balance of power in Europe and adjacent waters is, as the formation of the North Atlantic Alliance reveals, still a prerequisite for the West. But the European balance is now merely a key sector in a larger global balance.

One major prop of that global balance has been the naval preponderance which the West enjoys. There have not only been sea lanes to police in a traditional way. For a number of years the Western deterrent has been sea-based as well as land-based. And this last fact also may explain why, even when there is hostility on Soviet frontiers with China, unrest among European client states and all that NATO must withstand in Central Europe, a countervailing naval effort still figures among Soviet priorities.

After World War II the United States pitted against the further development of Soviet land-power a global nuclear apparatus with oceanic ramifications. Russia may get far without neutralising these. If she neutralises them she may get still further.

Such a dual Soviet aim could potentially become the gravest threat since Hitler to a free world order. And when the United States meets it, her British ally, in spite of severe budgetary constraints, has a particular contribution to make.

None has been as apt as Britain to preconcert far afield with others and that, as a residual propensity, is what might still guide her. It may not be innate but she had to live it down before General de Gaulle would have let her enter the Common Market. What he resented in Britain was all she still derived from Commonwealth bonds and her ultimate solidarity with the United States – the legacy, in short, of her oceanic past.

If the European Community is to attain its goal, moreover, there must be economic and political unification. In a full organic union with European neighbours Britain would accordingly have to abandon overseas sources of strength. She could have external links that other federalised components share and no others.

What Britain requires is an alternative that will restore some of the economic scope she once had without stultifying her politically. This she might achieve by a looser trading arrangement with the European Community or by a multilateral free trade area which extends far beyond the West European segment of the free world. If that kind of project could be organised it would enable Britain to prolong such overseas connections as may still help her to make her mark. But nothing can be done along those broader lines unless the United States recognises the utility to her, from a politico-strategic as well as an economic standpoint, of such a venture and, as leader of the West, takes an appropriate initiative.

Through the entry of Britain and others, at any rate, the enlargement of the European Community might revive the Gaullist drift towards a Third Force Europe – one that would divide the West at a conjuncture when its unity, with an American leader harassed by war in Indochina and hampered by manifold distractions at home, has seldom been so imperative. Certainly by merging her political identity with that of others in a close-knit European union, Britain would be sounding the death-knell of an oceanic grouping such as the Commonwealth and be doing it just when the maritime phase of the global contest between Russia and the West might render it more hazardous to keep safe that everyday traffic between Continents which civilised society takes for granted.

The nature of the Commonwealth has determined the effect which naval advances by the Soviet Union have had upon it. An oceanic Commonwealth could never have emerged if first Britain and then the United States had not kept the seas open for open societies. Among Afro-Asian members of the Commonwealth few abide by that heritage of law and public life which the British left behind. Yet the imponderables of the Commonwealth, at once so creative and so elusive, should not be minimised. They have set the higher political standards of open societies as those towards which a number of less open ones may still aspire.

Nor are such intangibles the Commonwealth's sole merit. There are trade pacts and programmes of financial and technical assistance. It was, moreover, by importing cheap foodstuffs from Commonwealth countries that Britain obtained export advantages which, upon entry into the Common Market, she would have to renounce. Even in concrete economic terms Britain should therefore have regarded the Commonwealth tie as a boon.

Irritants abound. It is, nevertheless, a tribute as well as a handicap when partners insist that Britain observe a stricter code of conduct than the rest. For Commonwealth transactions, she remains the centre. And as long as she does, she will, for a country of her size and resources, discharge a function that is globally unique.

Even so, none of this will be worth much if Britain's oceanic security is undermined by Russia's maritime endeavour to outflank the European sector of the global balance – if overseas partners of the Commonwealth are cut off from Britain and from each other.

After World War II when the American Sixth Fleet spread a protective wing over southern Europe its aircraft also had the Black Sea ports of the Soviet Union within reach. More recently it has had to reconcile itself to an offsetting Mediterranean presence by the Red Fleet – one from which Russia has reaped immense strategic profit. In the spring of 1967, after egging on her belligerent Egyptian ward, the Soviet Union could not save Egypt from a pre-emptive strike by Israel. Subsequently, however, the most up-to-date aircraft and anti-missile devices, with ten or fifteen thousand Soviet personnel and technicians, were sent to Egypt; the Soviet Navy has also obtained facilities at Alexandria and Port Said (as well as at Latakia in Syria). The Red Fleet, moreover, possesses helicopter carriers which can be modified, but no attack aircraft carriers. From the airfield at Cairo West it gets instead land-based air support which Russia may also procure elsewhere.

Some years later, when Egypt pared down the privileges she had given Russia, there was a treaty between the Soviet Union and Libya.

Throughout the Mediterranean this amphibious Soviet build-up has stirred apprehension. There are even misgivings over what Malta, a Commonwealth country, may do. For that island is a key to maritime communications between the

Eastern and Western Mediterranean. Her naval facilities, a bequest from Britain, could be at Russia's disposal if, following a change of government, the Maltese went neutralist. The same might occur, moreover, on the European littoral of the Mediterranean and then NATO would have fewer and fewer bases on its southern flank. Already as paymaster of the Arab cause, the Soviet Union may have got a footing at Mers el-Kebir, the former French base in Algeria. It could thus have both ends of the Mediterranean within its orbit.

The spirit Moscow exhibits is one of effrontery tempered by caution. As long as there is a European standstill between Russia and the West, the Soviet naval presence in the Mediterranean does not have to match in size the Mediterranean vigil that the American Sixth Fleet, with the navies of European allies, has been mounting. What it does do more immediately is fulfil an age-old Russian dream by serving as a cover for a Soviet breakthrough from the Middle East to the Indian Ocean.

Such a breakthrough would contrast with trends elsewhere. In Eastern and Central Europe, Russia has been consolidating the status quo and she is for it also in East and South Asia. She is, on the other hand, against the status quo in the Middle East as far as she may thereby promote her own interests rather than those of Arab client states or of Palestinian terrorists with a pro-Chinese orientation.

Important, above all, will be the extent to which the Russians penetrate the Persian Gulf in the wake of any Western withdrawal and after the Suez Canal has been unblocked. Russia may or may not want to extract and distribute the oil of the region. What she might covet is the ability to have it withheld in a showdown from Britain, other West European countries and Japan.

Even now, Russia has a grip on the Yemeni port of Hodeida, while in Somalia across the mouth of the Red Sea she is carving out an East African foothold. After Egypt had to retire from the Yemen and Britain withdrew from South Yemen Russia could bring the naval base and airport of Aden, together with the island of Socotra, within her clutches. Nor has she bagged any strategic prize as precious as this since she riveted her sway upon Eastern Europe. By operating from Aden and Socotra the Russians will traverse the Indian Ocean with ease.

For thus traversing it the Soviet Navy is also ensconced elsewhere. Russian fisheries and submarine fleets may collaborate and on behalf of the former, it is often reported, the Soviet Union has even signed agreements with Asian members of the Commonwealth. India denies that Russia has the use of naval facilities at Visakhapatam on her east coast or the Andaman and Nicobar Islands. What may be conjectured, rather, has been the use of those islands for exercises by the Royal Navy – a relic of long-recognised custom and Commonwealth bonds. And it would be reassuring if this were so. From Indian territories on the Bay of Bengal, Soviet naval vessels might command traffic, the heaviest in the world, passing through the Malacca Straits to and from Singapore and Malaysia up to Hong Kong and Japan.

Then Russia may be forging ahead off the coast of East Africa, nearer the Cape of Good Hope. The island of Mauritius, where there is a British naval radio relay station, has given facilities to Russian merchant ships (together with airport rights for Aeroflot) as well as to Soviet fishing trawlers. On the African mainland, Tanzania, another Commonwealth country, is also said to have a fisheries arrangement with Russia. And privileges like these might be converted later into something less innocuous.

It has long been patent that control of Egypt would provide Russia with a stepping-stone for the pursuit in the Indo-Pacific theatre of a still wider global strategy. The Truman Doctrine was devised to curtail any downward Soviet thrust through Greece and Turkey. In 1956, however, when Sir Anthony Eden and M. Guy Mollet might have impeded the Russian leapfrog across the Mediterranean, Washington did what it could to impede them – a self-defeating blow from which American policy in the Middle East has never recovered. Israel, with aircraft from the United States and yet with scant backing from other natural allies in the West, might again save herself from the perils by which she is beset. But there has also been the question whether an attempt will be made beyond the vicinity of the Suez Canal to take peripheral defence measures at the sea passages around the Cape of Good Hope and South-East Asia.

The answers, pro or con, have been ones for Britain also to find, and she has had to find them in a Commonwealth context. Nor can they be the same. In South-East Asia a cluster of other Commonwealth countries sought to persuade Britain to stay on when she tried to depart. At the Cape of Good Hope, the African members of the Commonwealth demanded that she leave.

The second closure of the Suez Canal, a by-product of the Six Day War between Israel and Arab states in 1967 was what provoked the Commonwealth crisis over the defence of the sea passage around the Cape of Good Hope. The longer route has been more costly for all ships, but Russia has not only had the extra roubles to consider. Other countries have been employing supertankers for the transportation of oil from the Persian Gulf which are precluded by their size from use of Suez and must therefore go around the Cape. The Soviet Union refrains, however, from building such monsters as they cannot navigate the straits of the Black and Baltic Seas or slice through ice that, for much of the year, obstructs the Arctic passage above Norway. Then, too, when Russian supplies for North Vietnam were debarred from travel across Chinese territory, the Soviet Union had to ship them by the slower haul around the Cape. And it would have to do the same if the trans-Siberian railway were exposed to bombing by a Chinese foe – unless the Suez Canal were available.

There was yet another war between Israelis and Arab States in October 1973. Through subsequent mediation by Secretary Kissinger, Israel withdrew from the two banks of the Suez Canal and Egypt, with Anglo-American assistance, could therefore undertake to clear that maritime and naval artery. Russia helped clear the Gulf of Suez and is building a second railway across Siberia.

The number of warships and submarines which Russia assigns to the Mediterranean might fluctuate. What they also do, nevertheless, is serve as a check upon that sea-air branch of the Western deterrent which, with allies, has the American Sixth Fleet as an unacknowledged escort. And now the Soviet Navy, even though to a much smaller degree, may watch the Indian Ocean with the same objective in mind. When, moreover, there is speedier access to it, Russia, protecting her own shorter route to East Asia, might, with land-based facilities, cast a shadow over the entire region.

Nor has assistance from within the Commonwealth been lacking. Politically this is the most permissive of entities and concessions made to Russian sea-power by Commonwealth members in the Indian Ocean must puzzle beneficiaries as politically unpermissive as the masters of the Kremlin.

It is a danger, moreover, which stems from a deepening solicitude in the West for the safety of sea traffic around South Africa. Today, quite apart from what happens to the Suez Canal, the Cape route has more than a fall-back utility. It is the only feasible path for giant tankers laden with much of that oil from the Middle East to which, like Japan, Britain and the rest of Western Europe have now geared their economies.

There are some, nevertheless, who wonder whether fortification of the Cape route is not strategically futile. The argument is that non-Soviet traffic will be in less jeopardy here than elsewhere because the Cape is so far from the North Atlantic where roving Soviet marauders would have nearby havens of their own and where, so as to contain the Soviet naval menace, NATO is also better off.

This might well be so – though Russian detachments may get afloat support, that modern method of supply. But it is not only the West with which the Soviet Union competes; there is also the advent to Zambia and Tanzania of the Communist Chinese. Far beyond Sino-Soviet frontiers, Moscow combats Maoist ideology and its fascination for non-white peoples by Chinese forward strides in war technology. Russia thus has yet another motive for showing the flag off the coast of East Africa. By doing so she may augment Soviet political inroads. If there are ensuing grants of naval facilities, these will increase the Russian strategic capacity among the sea lanes of the region.

South Africa, with the most convenient of sites for surveillance over the Cape route, has been willing to undertake that mission. It is one which Britain, by renewing the sale of naval arms to the Republic, wanted to foster. But some overseas members of the Commonwealth have not been as ready to acquiesce in sales of that kind to South Africa.

For a number of years Britain ensured the defence of the area through an agreement with South Africa under which British naval vessels could be berthed and fuelled at the Simonstown base or use other South African ports. The (first) Wilson government, however, banned the sale of arms to South Africa after the Security Council of the United Nations denounced that country in 1963 for its cruel mistreatment of blacks by whites. Since then the politico-strategic picture has altered. The Heath government ran, all the same, into a hornet's nest when they proposed to lift the embargo.

Commonwealth capitals opposed to such a proceeding contended that South Africa could employ British naval arms to reinforce the iniquities of apartheid and it is indeed true that some of those weapons might have more than one use. In 1956, when the British and French attempted to re-occupy Suez, Afro-Asian quarters reverberated with threats of secession from the Commonwealth and Ottawa asked London to desist. It did the same again.

Not that Afro-Asian countries are habitually averse to political compromise. Many forgive the West its sins lest worse befall; some, doubting that anything could be worse, condone transgressions by antagonists of the West with singular alacrity. But when countries like India and Pakistan now do this, it is because they have axes of their own to grind.

The British *raj*, with its Asian sphere of influence, had long averted any territorial push by the Russians down to the Indian sub-continent. Until the eve of World War I there was also British naval predominance to prevent Tsarist Russia, so repressive and predatory on land, from penetrating the Indo-Pacific theatre by sea. Today, when most other empires have been liquidated, the Soviet imperium – diminished territorially by World War I and territorially reaggrandised by World War II – seizes the opportunity for expansion by sea beyond its own Eurasian domains. Anti-imperialist countries like India and Pakistan are thus put within a Russian ambit at last. It is, all the same, Communist China, the scourge of Tibet, that does most to couple together, as miscreants, the resurgent imperialism of Russia with the defunct imperialism of the West. For India has been eager to cultivate Russia as a counterpoise against China and against Pakistan over Kashmir.

1971 saw another war between India and Pakistan but now the setting of diplomacy had been revamped. Bangladesh seceded, under Indian auspices, from Pakistan. India was backed by Russia while Pakistan, when the United States was seeking a detente with China, had support (to no avail) from both Peking and Washington.

It is a tangled skein. Until the Organisation of African Unity was aroused the French went on selling arms to South Africa (while black states of Francophone Africa have also been trading with the Boer Republic) and those sales may not wholly cease. In addition, after Britain announced her strategic withdrawals from the Indian Ocean and the South Atlantic there was a *rapprochement* between South Africa and the two chief powers of Latin America, Brazil and Argentina, with the object of making the waters of the South Atlantic more secure. Brasilia and Buenos Aires, removed as they are from African and Commonwealth affairs, might be suitable intermediaries for South Africa if she purchases naval arms abroad. Their procurement through West European channels should also relieve Britain while oceanically the West will be no weaker.

On unreason, after all, Afro-Asian countries have no monopoly. In their case the wounds of racism account for much. And one outcome may be that Britain's own investments and export drive will suffer if, by furnishing South Africa with naval arms, she invites trade reprisals within the Commonwealth from some of her African partners.

Strategically, too, prudence is ordained. Against the day when the Cairo-Moscow axis might seek to exclude military aircraft of the West from the airspace of the Middle East, Britain will have to maintain a more circuitous route for air communications with Commonwealth countries of South-East Asia and the Antipodes. A modicum of goodwill among the Commonwealth nations in Africa is therefore essential if Britain is to retain those air or landing rights with which British staging posts in the Indian Ocean would be the other intercontinental links. And she has, above all, a still more imminent contingency to anticipate. It would serve no rational defence purpose if, by selling arms to South Africa, Britain so alienated some African countries that they retaliated by offering naval facilities to the Soviet Union.

The auguries are such as to suggest that Britain would do better for herself and for the West if, on this most bedevilled of topics, she bowed out. It is not one over which the Commonwealth, with its value to the free world as a whole, should run the risk of a deeper rift or even of breaking up.

Meanwhile, to the north of the Indian Ocean, pressure of a very different sort has been exerted upon Britain. There, intent upon the security of South-East Asia, Commonwealth countries were piqued by a British pullback rather than by a reassertion of limited involvement. Henceforth, according to a new defence policy enunciated in the late 1960s, Britain was to devote herself chiefly to the European sector of the global balance. Ministers blamed economic stress for the nation's disengagement East of Suez. With the change of administration during 1970, however, Britain started to entertain the idea of a more substantial commitment in South East Asia. Malaysia and Singapore should feel less insecure if the British contribute to a joint security arrangement between five Commonwealth Powers, Britain, Malaysia, Singapore, Australia and New Zealand. And what this cannotes is that, even if it is a modest one, Britain will stick to her presence in the Indian Ocean. It is, above all, what the situation East of Suez calls for.

By the middle of the 1970s, nevertheless, expenditure on Britain's own defence, through the North Atlantic Alliance, had to come before outlying commitments – though even France, semi-isolated as she has been, will station an aircraft carrier in that zone. Britain's contribution to Anzuk, the Commonwealth force in Singapore, may not last very long. But there is still a British island facility in the Indian Ocean which she can share with the United States.

Will France or the USA become residuary legatee if Britain lets the Simonstown treaty wither on the vine? The trends are such in Western and Southern Europe that, for the oceanic strategy of the West, the French may be no more staunch than they have been nearer home. Nowadays, as Washington must perceive, the choice of ports and the deployment of warships should keep company with other things.

Over this there may well have been qualms in Washington. It has long been imbued with the curiously schizoid notion that, even after Britain is Europeanised, she will contrive somehow to blend the Eurocentric with the extra-European. In July 1967 President Johnson expressed hope that the British would not withdraw from East of Suez. What he contemplated, presumably, was tacit coordination between an American and British presence in the Indian Ocean. Since the early 1960s various ports on the coast of East Africa have received periodic visits from warships flying the Stars and Stripes – a naval unit of two destroyers with its flagship, an aircraft tender, based on Bahrein in the Persian Gulf.

NATO itself is menaced, though, if Norway shares control of Spitsbergen with Russia and submarines pass, unobserved, from Murmansk to the North Atlantic.

The issue is plain. Not since the days of the German Emperor, William II, has a maritime rival flung down so prodigious a gauntlet. It was against a similar attempt to combine massive land-power with far-reaching naval and colonial aspirations that, at the turn of the century, Britain had been spurred into an alignment with Imperial Japan, Republican France and Tsarist Russia while also reinsuring herself with the United States. Nothing that the Japanese or Nazis undertook in the maritime realm after World War I was to be so all-encompassing. But what principally distinguishes the Soviet bid for naval supremacy from those earlier endeavours is its dual character – the search, that is to say, for an invincibility at sea in the old style, the new-style oceanic vehicles of the Western deterrent and the quest for their neutralisation.

The United States, with her allies, is still supreme at sea. And yet by his utterances Admiral Sergei Gorshkov, with the backing of the Soviet Defence Minister, Mr Andrei A.

Grechko, is more reminiscent of his German precursor, Admiral von Tirpitz, or so redoubtable an Edwardian sea-dog as Lord Fisher than of an American naval thinker of the period as notable as Captain Mahan. In two world wars the German Navy tried to split free societies from each other and, after Hitler flouted the Nazi-Soviet Pact, to segregate the embattled Russians from those in the West who brought succour by sea at so great a cost in men, shipping and supplies. Today, the Red Fleet might also want to split free societies from each other and, more even than the Red Army, enforce as law a Russian ukase where Russian power has never been exerted before.

Such a state of affairs can transform the world scene. Ever since World War II the United States and her allies have upheld a global balance from fulcra that are maritime as well as territorial. Nowadays, however, a Eurasian super-power is attaining leverage, like that which Britain and the United States have had, to intervene at will on other world fronts. Britain, after Trafalgar, and the United States, after she took Britain's place as the leader of the West, underwrote a free world order in which free nations survived as did many of the unfree who had the good fortune to dwell behind the shield of a benevolent oceanic preponderance. The preservation of that shield will be no simple task.

The new war technology prevents world war through a global balance while at the same time it enhances, short of nuclear war, much that is bellicose. Benefiting from an ensuing immunity, Russia has been castigating positions of strength, but if she and the West ever try to negotiate a world settlement, she can be in a stronger position herself.

As for Britain and other Commonwealth countries, there was a maritime element in whatever governed their common past and, as far as common ties are concerned, it will govern their common future no less. One test must be the degree to which the British people, after being the linch-pin of an oceanic aggregation, let themselves lapse into a mere outer island adjunct of continental land-power. Britain will be Europeanised only if she has lost faith in herself. But she may lose more than that if open societies do not manage to keep open the open seas.

14 The Enlargement of the European Community and its Global Effects*

Can the West afford to experiment with its own make-up at a time when it has a global contest on its hands? More than a detente is required to ensure maximum security and without maximum security it should take no chances. The Atlantic nexus relies, after all, on much beyond the Atlantic and much beyond the Atlantic relies on it.

World politics, with the advent of long-range weapons and the movement of power to massive centres beyond Western Europe, have acquired a new global dimension that Western Europe itself may treat ambiguously. The European Economic Community hankers, through enlargement, for the higher status of super-power. Even though that entity cannot attain such a rank by its own unaided efforts, it might, by the manner in which it pursues its goal, impair the broader unity of the West.

What could portend was evident long before Washington began to toy with an hypothesis suited to a period of American retrenchment, one upon which others have leaped so wishfully. It is predicated upon the illusion that there will be less for the United States and the Soviet Union to do when the labels of super-power are pinned on China, Japan and a bigger European Community. Yet such labels, as China and Japan have sensed, must be earned in all branches of power. As for the European Community, it has been making its mark as an economic giant but in no other category. And that is a disability of which even now it is only half aware.

As Japan adjusts herself to politico-strategic realities she may feel her way by trial and error. Champions of an enlarged Community are neither as modest in their approach nor as tentative. What they covet are the prerogatives of a

*This essay was first published as an article in *Pacific Community* (Tokyo, Apr 1972). There have been a few minor alterations, and some redundant passages have been eliminated.

super-power. But there are also functions which go with this high rank and to those less heed is paid.

It is scarcely news that Britain's entry is what will do most to enlarge the European Community. Her own residual scope though might not be enlarged, as many imagine, but narrowed. A process may start with reverberations that resound throughout the free world. How they do so is what will be examined here.

If Britain ever had to choose between Europe and the open sea, in the classic phrase attributed by Charles de Gaulle to Winston Churchill, she will choose the open sea. So historic a dictum was spurned, however, when a successor of Churchill's, Mr Edward Heath, visited M. Georges Pompidou, a successor of de Gaulle's, in May 1971. Not until the one informed the other that Britain was ready to turn from the open sea and make herself fast to the adjacent continent did she get the green light for entry into the European Community. Nor were the omens auspicious for so epoch-making a shift. Lines of oceanic communication between scattered units of the free world are more threatened nowadays by Soviet maritime expansion than they have been since the era of Kaiser William II and Admiral von Tirpitz. Without parallel has been a British knack for preconcerted exertions with the United States and Commonwealth countries across the seas. Britain, nevertheless, will forfeit lingering vestiges of this as her reorientation occurs. So, too, as the European Community pulls away from the United States, it might encourage the latter to pull away from it. The power structure of the West could thus be fragmented at a juncture when its antagonists would be as pleased as ever to see that happen. And the question remains whether there will still be time, with or without the European Community, for the West to take steps over a wide scale which might abate, if they do not forestall, the wide damage that may be wrought.

Much depends on the Community's size. If it includes Britain, most of non-Soviet Europe, with minor exceptions, will hasten to join. So pell-mell a rush could render the Community ungovernable. Against such chaos, nevertheless, the case for administrative centralisation would be all the more cogent. In their memorable talks of May 1971, M. Georges Pompidou, President of France, and Mr Edward Heath, Prime

Minister of Britain, contemplated a limited confederal project that will have room for an economic and monetary union. What they did not appreciate was that there can be no limits of the kind they entertained when economic and monetary union is undertaken. Outright political unification has had, in Herr Willy Brandt, Chancellor of the Community's most affluent segment, a staunch advocate. And this is what, in accordance with American and Imperial German precedents, will tend, sooner or later, to prevail.

It was, after all, through political as well as economic unification that the United States, despite grave flaws in her system of representative democracy, pushed to the fore. Those who speak for a bigger Community hope it will do likewise. They may differ over methods. Only by endowing itself with the ramified modalities of statehood can an enlarged Community consolidate its own enlargement and forge ahead. Whether it is shoved from behind or led from the van it must adopt them inexorably.

Multifarious these will be. When the Americans first declared their independence they tried a decentralized union like the one M. Pompidou and Mr Heath endorsed in May 1971. It fell short. The United States suffered a hideous Civil War (discrepancies of language, race, traditions and living standards are not the same in Western Europe) before she could make headway as a genuine federal union. Bismarck, crushing the Hapsburgs and French with blood and iron, transformed a ramshackle Zollverein into a German-speaking federalised Empire. In the United States, besides, uniformity was imposed by the steam-roller of corporate bigness. The Executive, Congress and Supreme Court bicker without surcease to bring under a single rule of law much that is so intractable sectionally. It is, by tragic contrast, Canada's inability to weld herself together that mars her promise as a Middle Power. She lives under the shadow of an American mammoth. But even if she did not she would be handicapped fiscally and linguistically when varied clusters of so sparse a population dwell at so immense a distance from each other. A millennium of wars, however, is what has done most to keep Western Europe disunited and, as far as these were civil wars, they may never recur. It is on shuttles of trade that the warp and woof of Community fabric is being woven. Yet only behind the ramparts of the North Atlantic Alliance and the American nuclear deterrent could that economically federalising process go on unimpeded.

As hub of world politics, Western Europe cannot restore itself. The European Community proposes, though, still to be heard from and it has boosters with a self-assurance which the past of its main components, swinging as they have between the high-minded and iniquitous, refutes. Nobody knows how it will behave. Less in doubt is what it may be like. The unification of Western Europe stood little chance before technology could surmount obstacles of language and culture. Now it can. The Treaty of Rome, from which the Community derives, is slanted towards the organic and supra-national. Against a further pooling of national sovereignty the progenitors of the Community, lest it stagnate or collapse, dare not hold out indefinitely.

There must, all the same, be reminders of how it might still fall apart. Now or later Britain may not stay within the confines of the European Community. Others can and should. Yet unless there is the closest integration between them they will be unable, even from an administrative standpoint, to progress together.

None of this will be feasible, all the same, without major institutions in world politics and the world economy being reshaped. The French have insisted on a Eurocentric bent for Britain – the renunciation, that is, of overseas affinites, Commonwealth and Anglo-American. But it has always been apparent that components of a larger federalised union could never, in any case, retain external ties or conduct foreign policies of their own. As a unit that has been Europeanised, therefore, Britain will have to drop individual contacts with the United Nations, the North Atlantic Alliance and other international bodies. Only through the Community could she adhere to them – and neither she nor the free world in general can safely prophesy where, over contentious issues, that entity will always wind up.

For Britain, in addition, a gamble on Community membership will be more serious than it is for most other participants. Those with roots in the tangibles of land-power could recover speedily if the European Community should ever break down. Britain, sustained by intangibles of a more dispersed oceanic nature, cannot regain tomorrow what she abandons today. The age is one, furthermore, in which the ultimate criteria of world order are on a global scale and for it Britain's own widespread sources of strength were also well adapted geographically. She cannot finally jettison remnants of these without being enfeebled within Europe itself.

Those are subtle points and if Britain soft-pedalled them, the United States, since the days of the Marshall and Schuman Plans, was apt to gloss over them entirely. With American leadership of the West also came American primacy at sea but American power has had a continental mould. Washington took it for granted that the British, supported by the smaller democracies of Western Europe, would be able to stifle trends that were undemocratic, neutralist, protectionist or rabidly anti-American. Willy-nilly, however, Britain might be caught up in them. Overseas affiliations were her substitute for continental self-sufficiency and without these she cannot do much.

If Britain joined the European Community she could implement her view of world order only if most components shared it with her. The United States yearned for them to do so and persuaded herself that they would. She took Anglo-American amity as a premise while demanding a change in the conditions under which it could survive. Nor did she tolerate forebodings that transatlantic relations would be more and not less awkward to coordinate after the European Community is enlarged. Seldom can American policy be squared with American interests at once. On no other cardinal issue has the divergence lasted so long.

It is one, moreover, which major American opinion media have done all they could to foster. They are poised to dissect the Washington scene every hour on the hour. Yet the Europeanisation of Britain has been a subject they have seldom put in a broad global context. They pride themselves on being sentinels of free expression. From London, however, they have relayed without dissent whatever campaign arguments Westminster has planted on British counterparts. As in Britain they greeted most critical books with silence or usually misrepresented the few they did review. Most articles have had to follow a prescribed editorial line. Some of this bias could be traced back, perhaps, to directives from owners, executives and editors in New York and Washington with connections among top-level Europeanisers in Britain. It may also reflect the long arm of Jean Monnet, arch-propagandist of European union, and the clasp he has had on senior Washington officials from whom a number who write and broadcast for the American public get their cues. But whatever its origins there has been a transatlantic manipulation of opinion, at once so bland and so ruthless, into which copious research is waiting to be done. An enlargement of the European Community may have a split in the West as its outcome. So dire a result has not been unforeseen. The need, year after year and decade after decade, was for many-sided discussion. Tacit foreclosure has ensued.

The setting is thus an elusive one and so are specific overseas factors that Britain furthered globally. What will the free world lose if, upon her Europeanisation, these expire? Reference has been made to international bodies – the North Atlantic Alliance, the United Nations, those preoccupied more strictly with economic affairs – which henceforth would have to do without a British member; for which, on behalf of Britain, the European Community itself must serve as intermediary. Later, too, there will be comment about disruptive, anti-American, Eurocentric trends speeded up in a Community enlarged and unified through Britain's entry. But neither will the free world have cause to rejoice if the Commonwealth disintegrates and Anglo-American friendship dies away. As global factors these are *sui generis* and there has never been anything that can take their place.

About the Commonwealth, it may be argued, much has long tended towards self-liquidation. And yet that worldwide miscellany persists. It could not do so without some inner consensus, at once ill-defined and indefinable, that it should. As the Commonwealth evolved British dependencies could struggle for independence against the British themselves. A voluntary multiracial Commonwealth was the upshot.

As long as it perseveres, the Commonwealth will be a twentieth-century political phenomenon which, by any comparative estimate, is quite unique. There are also programmes of financial and technical assistance. And now developing countries of the Commonwealth in the Indian and Pacific Oceans, Africa and the Caribbean may obtain associate memberships from the European Community. They will not do that, however, as part of an historic aggregation. It was, besides, profitable for everyone concerned when Britain also imported cheap foodstuffs and raw materials from more developed Commonwealth partners – Canada, Australia and New Zealand. British exports gained thereby a competitive edge in world markets. Britain is to have instead direct access to the European Community with its exorbitant charges and levies. But even as the overall percentage of British trade with Commonwealth countries dwindled, the economics of the Commonwealth were still a boon.

More sensational have been grounds for disenchantment with Commonwealth ties. Britain has often been piqued when, during controversial episodes, Commonwealth partners have clamoured for her to abide by a stricter code of conduct than they set for themselves. Yet she would never have stamped herself upon the modern era – indeed at some junctures in two world wars she might have gone down to defeat – if she were not revivified by intangibles shared with others beyond the limits of her own small island and of her own European vicinity. For the people of Edmund Burke and Winston Churchill, a materialist and quasi-Marxian interpretation of history can thus scarcely be the whole story. It is a tribute, articulate or inarticulate, when so disparate an assortment of nations converges on a British focus voluntarily. And it should, despite provocations, be regarded as such.

This same point might be made in another way. While land-power binds through centralisation, a more decentralised scheme of things may flourish where the sea is a traditional link. And that is a truth about which the British, with Europeanisation as an objective, might conveniently forget. It was Canada that did most to work out equality of status as a concept through which the Commonwealth was somehow to endure. But when London puts the emphasis more and more on the Eurocentric, this will matter less and less.

One recent example may illustrate how confused the atmosphere is. For the security of Southeast Asia and so as to renew her presence East of Suez against the Soviet challenge at sea, Britain signed in 1971 a consultative pact with four overseas Commonwealth partners of the region – Australia, New Zealand, Malaysia and Singapore. But when she concluded this agreement she was also dickering with the Six over terms upon which they would let her join the European Community. As an enlarged Community verges on unification, Britain's presence within it may jar with her presence East of Suez. Thereupon Britain could propose no doubt that, as political Europe becomes a single entity, its British component might serve as its agent. The assumption would be that Britain and the Community will always cherish the same world view and express the same politico-strategic outlook. It is not a safe one to make. What should also be remembered is that the more Western Europe is unified the less can each component retain sufficient command of the purse-strings to chart with others, in remote corners of the earth, any course of its own.

Nor is it only the Commonwealth phase of the British role that the Europeanisation of Britain would stultify and extinguish. There is that Anglo-American friendship upon which Winston Churchill and Franklin Delano Roosevelt were to lay an impress but which began to lay its own impress on world politics at the turn of the century. The German Reich, underwriting the restive empire of the Hapsburgs, had to be resisted when its bid for hegemony, not unlike that of contemporary Russia, arrayed might on land with universal ambitions in other politico-strategic domains. As splendid isolation ceased to be splendid Britain gravitated towards Imperial Japan, Republican France and Tsarist Russia. Concurrently, as so many historians still do not grasp, the British also reinsured themselves with the United States. An Anglo-American factor thus emerged and for free peoples during the first half of the twentieth century this was to be the most momentous of realignments.

Since World War II, however, many among the British have fancied that they might find an escape across the Channel from the disproportion in strength between the two main English-speaking countries. But instead of doing better they will only do worse. There has, as a matter of fact, been nothing unusual about such disproportions in strength between the United States and Britain. The Anglo-American framework lacked symmetry before the United States took

Britain's place as leader of the West. It was when Britannia ruled the waves that, unmolested, the young American Republic could build itself up within its own continental boundaries and beyond. Still exceptional about Britain is a flair, acquired in her heyday, for cooperating far afield with others. The retraction of that practice has been forecast, nevertheless, by the accord which Messrs Pompidou and Heath reached in May 1971 for a British shift from the oceanic to the Eurocentric. Unhesitatingly the French thereupon lifted their veto on Britain's entry into the European Community. Through Community membership, moreover, a diversion by her from overseas to continental priorities will have a constitutional aftermath. And so, as during the 1930s, a British élite may again have misjudged the most vital of national interests. Nor did the United States, despite global yardsticks which her own primacy requires, find fault. It has long been gospel in Washington that, even after their Europeanisation, the British will discover nothing incompatible between the Eurocentric and the extra-European. States of the Union have no rights abroad. For Britain, all the same, Washington had still postulated range for manoeuvre.*

This is an anomaly of which the future must take care. In

*It has been the present writer's view from the outset that there was a clash between the politico-strategic interests of the Atlantic world and any enlargement of the European Community which absorbed Britain. If Western Europe thus became an anti-American, neutralist Third Force, the power structure of the West would be undercut.

An article by the writer in the *Statist* (London, 9 March 1962) pp. 728-9, suggested that Washington should ask members of the Common Market to make some allowance for world-wide British needs: 'A better safeguard for the West than a tight union in Western Europe would be a loose union in which Britain can still bring her weight to bear. She may have varied interests to reconcile. But so, as a whole, has the West.'

After a new American Trade Expansion Bill had been passed and before the first Gaullist veto, the writer proposed yet another American trade initiative. *Monthly Bulletin* (Commonwealth Industries Association, London, Dec 1962) pp. 7-8.

Charles de Gaulle vetoed British entry in January 1963. The writer reiterated a post-veto case for a new American trade initiative, from the politico-strategic angle, in *Orbis* (Spring 1963) pp. 250-64.

For a recapitulation and broader general estimate: Lionel Gelber, *The Alliance of Necessity* (Stein and Day, New York, 1966; Robert Hale Ltd, London, 1967) pp. 31-40, 122-40, 158-88.

the meantime strategic weapons have been sea-based as well as land-based and, between scattered parts of the free world, there are oceanic communications to patrol. London and Washington have therefore been erecting joint Anglo-American defence facilities at Diego Garcia, an island of the British Indian Ocean Territories. These, moreover, might also lend themselves to trips by submarines, American or British, with long-range missiles and which, from the Arabian Sea, might have Russia's own home soil as a target for deterrence.

Even now American warships have access to staging posts on British atolls in the region while, with British ones, they might still dock at Cockburn Sound, a naval base planned in Western Australia by Australia, ally of the United States under the ANZUS pact and cosignatory with Britain of the new Commonwealth security pact for Southeast Asia. What may also be observed is how, after President Nixon visited the Sixth Fleet in 1970, he greeted a further British presence not only in the Mediterranean but also East of Suez.

Improved American facilities (logistic, sea and air) at the British island of Diego Garcia should compensate in the Indian Ocean for the growth of Soviet naval activities as these encroach, together with the reopening of the Suez Canal, upon Southern Asia and East Africa. India complained, however, that through such countervailing American moves the Indian Ocean was being converted into a zone of superpower competition. But in Aden, Somalia and Iraq, as President Ford insisted, Russia already had three operating bases. About these New Delhi kept mum.

The West, however, had long been conversant with Indian casuistry. According to this India's long stride towards an atomic bomb will not be abused, nor must others do as she did when she fastened her grip on Sikkim more firmly. Thus, too, as she pleaded for fertiliser and grain from the United States, she never acknowledged that what aggravated famine, with a populace that teemed so excessively, was extortion by oil States. Pro-Arab, none the less, she remained. But echoes of Indian jeremiads also came from the Antipodes.

When, however, Australia and New Zealand remonstrated against a superpower built-up in the Indian Ocean, their protests went to Moscow as well as Washington. The security of Australasia hinges, all the same, on the Anzus Pact. The better the United States can enforce this regionally the safer the West, as a whole, will be.

The French, though, were more specific when, with naval bases, they augmented their fleet in the Indian Ocean. They, too, were against superpower predominance over sea lanes on which oil for Western Europe is transported from the Persian Gulf. Yet like Australasia's commitment to the United States, France, as a signatory of the North Atlantic Alliance, had not disavowed her choice between rival concepts of world order. And whatever fortifies the West in one oceanic theatre enables others to do more elsewhere.

The United States, torn between domestic burdens and post-Viet Nam reluctance to comport herself as a global gendarme, cannot stand guard everywhere. The American Seventh Fleet and the Soviet Pacific Fleet keep watch on the Chinese coastline as well as on each other. When the Soviet Navy makes its bid for parity or ascendancy, the Western Pacific and Mediterranean (apart from the American Second Fleet stationed in the Atlantic and the American First Fleet in the Eastern Pacific) continue as decisive theatres in the American calculus of global sea power. But others, too, must take account of the huge interconnecting zone of the Indian Ocean.

To do that, however, is also to scrutinise the effect of an enlarged European Community beyond Europe. For Western Europe itself a bigger edifice is not necessarily a better one. Without being enlarged, the Community is, as a trading bloc, numbered already among the titans of the earth. And yet when it is centralised or federalised it may be no model of representative democracy as the British people themselves understand that type of governance. The European Commission, with a writ authorised by the Treaty of Rome, has provoked scepticism. A confederal scheme for a Parliament of Parliaments, as visualised in May 1971 by Messrs Pompidou and Heath, cannot last. More serious is incertitude, nurtured by their records, over the democratic stability of major components. The Bonn Republic has enjoyed prosperity but has never had to weather the storms that shook the Weimar Republic from the outset. In France, as recently as 1968, even that Gaullist régime which still praises itself as immune to the hereditary defects of French democracy, was nearly overthrown. In Italy where, as in France, the Communists form the largest political party, there is not only civil strife with neo-fascists; in both countries the extreme Left expounds neutralist foreign policies (Italy being next door to the neutralist Yugoslavs) which, if adopted, could in themselves menace NATO's southern flank. Britain cannot avoid strains and stresses that afflict the Western Alliance as a whole. She could aggravate them for herself, however, by more intimate Community links.

Mature political behaviour for such an entity has, nevertheless, been deemed axiomatic by its architects and proponents. Mr Heath had to show his credentials as a good European when he visited the Elysée Palace in May 1971 and before others among the Six were permitted by its Presidential occupant to complete negotiations for Britain's entry. One point made by the Prime Minister after he had been awarded full marks in Paris was that he and the President of France seek a Europe which will deal on a basis of equality with the United States, Japan or the Soviet Union in trade, finance and 'the use of influence.' But there are grave doubts over how that influence may be used. It might therefore be no misfortune if, as a weightier vehicle in world politics, the European Community still cannot presume to exercise the same global influence as a full-fledged super-power. First, at all events, it must display more prowess in a domain as decisive as defence. Shored up within NATO by the conventional weapons of the United States as well as by fear among adversaries of the American nuclear deterrent, it is now a giant with a limp. The question is though whether, lopsided and partially incapacitated, it will not still be big enough partially to incapacitate its own American guarantor.

The United States took in her stride a Gaullist predilection, one muted by M. Pompidou, for equating an American super-power, by whom the defence of Western Europe is upheld, with a Russian super-power against whom this very job has to be done. The European Community itself, all the same, cannot rate as a super-power when another of that rank must underwrite its security. But as a sub-superpower (the Chinese term applied to India) it could, from its important strategic position and with its economic pre-eminence, still dislocate the power structure of the West. Nor will a *détente* that is rash be the same as the one that is well-conceived. The Kremlin desires Western Europe to go off on its own and so, within bounds, does that Gaullism to which, with M. Pompidou, Mr Heath had long been so prone. Though unison in defence was the purpose of the last *Entente Cordiale* its resurrection is broached. And what should be recollected is that a celebrated predecessor also had as its sequel a Triple Entente in which the third participant was Russia.

Since the British people may owe their new Europeanised status to the Anglo-French rapprochement, it is proper to ask whether friction with France can be evaded. London must grapple with antithetical commitments under the institutional accord of May 1971 between Messrs Pompidou and Heath. For while the President and the Prime Minister believed that Community membership involved no erosion of national sovereignty, they also approved of a project for economic and monetary union through which national sovereignty must steadily be eroded. In any case, by fathering super-power pretensions, Messrs Pompidou and Heath have set forth other Community aims which cannot be fulfilled without political union. These might be attained, moreover, only when every branch of Community defence comes under a single rule. French and British nuclear deterrents would thus have to be merged before the Community is authentically one. Britain, though, has obtained classified nuclear information from the United States. Washington cannot withhold this from France if, for the political unification of Western Europe, there is genuine American backing.

All may prefer to let sleeping dogs lie. But that will be impracticable if, by the Community's sheer inner logic, the demand for effective governance drives it towards unification. As things are the French can avail themselves of routine American facilities even if American nuclear secrets are withheld. But they have regarded their deterrent as a counterweight to manifestations of West German regional supremacy and it could no longer serve as that after the Community has been unified. With others a component like the Bonn Republic would be entitled to a finger on the nuclear trigger. Nor should Moscow balk – though it might have done so before *Ostpolitik* gave it an opportunity for a *Westpolitik* of its own. The Kremlin may rue the day that it introduced China to nuclear weaponry. American and Russian superpowers might impose curbs upon critical segments of the arms race. A merged Community deterrent, however, may become another device for detaching Western Europe from North America. This Gaullist propensity might be a hidden, latent one. Russia could still utilise it for predatory, schismatic purposes of her own.

Not that Moscow will hail every aspect of such a change. Hitherto, as British nuclear weapons were coordinated with the overall American deterrent, there has been within the West a relatively stabilised nuclear control. Henceforth, if a merged Community deterrent moves from a single-handed American control, everybody would be somewhat less secure. And so here again the enlargement of the European Community may have a wide negative effect. If it undoes Atlantic solidarity, it might also undo much more.

Nor is this the only sphere in which, as the Community is enlarged and unified, the problem of defence would be less easy. Components will also have to merge their commitments to the North Atlantic Alliance. And that is a step to which the French may again be more averse than the British. Though France still adheres to the Alliance itself, she evicted the military branch of NATO, its functional apparatus, and thus provoked the departure of NATO's political high command. There must be more than mere routine cooperation with NATO if, after thus multiplying the costs of the Alliance and lessening its capacity, she is to make amends.

France did what she could to disrupt the territorial integrity of Canada – an Atlantic ally that, twice in this century, had gone to her rescue. At last, tardily and listlessly, France has seen ahead breakers long visible in the Western Mediterranean. During 1956 the British and French together, hindered by Messrs Eisenhower, Dulles and Hammarskjöld, might still have slowed up the conversion of the Middle East into a springboard for a long Soviet jump into Afro-Asian and Indo-Pacific theatres. Nothing did more than American impolicy during the Suez venture, among many who aspersed as well as some who vindicated Sir Anthony Eden, to imbue the nascent European Community with a muffled anti-American rationale. But Gaullist diplomacy stood on its head when it tried thereafter to throw Russia into the global balance against a leader of the West even as misguided as the United States had been.

In an alliance more than its author suffers from a national policy which is self-defeating. Exponents claim that the defence of the West will be revitalised by an enlargement of the European Community. It will, by some dispiriting auguries, only be devitalised.

Like Washington, Paris favours a European security conference but it objects to any scheme for mutually balanced force reductions which pare down the West European presence of the United States. Yet a lag in sharing NATO burdens with the United States and in matching ominous increases by the Warsaw Pact is being tackled by the Eurogroup of the North Atlantic Alliance – a West European caucus with Britain and the Bonn Republic in the lead and with France still a conspicuous absentee. But none of these activities now concern the European Community as such. They may do so only when, upon its unification, they must be funnelled through it. And even then the performance of France on the world stage will have to improve before the North Atlantic Alliance can rely upon the European Community as an instrument of policy.

But there is more than her contumacy over defence to hamper the Anglo-French rapprochement. For over a decade the British Establishment has presupposed that when Britain enters the European Community she will have the assistance of junior components in holding the reins. The French themselves, on the other hand, have stipulated that Britain dissever overseas ties so that she might devote herself within the Community to keeping France on top. Unlike the British, nevertheless, France could still fall back on her assiduous

Francophonie (one that spreads from French-speaking Africa to French-speaking Quebec) and which could, as after Bismarck's triumph, be yet another diversion from the Rhine. But what might give all this an air of unreality is that, while components of the Community may fret over whether the French or West Germans come first within it, few elsewhere will do so. The whole of Western Europe is nowadays merely a key sector in a global equilibrium which, for her own security, the United States must still maintain and by which the old European balance of power has been supplanted. What matters about that sector is how and with what, beyond Western Europe, an enlarged Community may be tempted to combine.

More perplexing than the vacillations of the French could be an historic German ambivalence between East and West. Behind *Ostpolitik* lies that interaction of European and Asian affairs which has been so constant a feature of world politics since the end of the nineteenth century and the early years of the twentieth. Tension between Russia and China must have crystallised Moscow's resolve to prevent the reappearance of a strong German neighbour on the European frontiers of the Soviet *imperium*. Eurasian power realities have thus compelled Bonn to defer provisionally – permanently, however, if East Germany obeys Muscovite decrees – its quest for the reunification of the two Germanies. But, like the three Soviet votes in the General Assembly of the United Nations, one loophole remains. Others assent to a pan-Arab mystique under which sovereign Arab states proclaim themselves fragments of a single Arab nation. So also, when the Bonn Republic deems itself no more than a separate part of the German nation as a whole, the last stigmata of pan-Germanism have yet to be erased.

For the time being, nevertheless, the global interests of the West have been served. If the re-emergence of a greater Germany distracted Russia from the affairs of East Asia there would be less to check the resurgent Chinese from extending their jurisdiction. The plight of Tibet might be repeated. And when Russia is the one that sticks to the partition of the late-Victorian Reich, Bonn can scarcely conspire with Moscow in the vein of Rapallo and the Nazi-Soviet Pact.

Ostpolitik may be accompanied, however, by economic concomitants. Through these, as they fit into a selective tactic of *détente* for Western Europe, Russia could perhaps still achieve politico-strategic mastery of the region after all. *Ostpolitik* might thus bring about a contingency which, with other Western policies, it is designed to ward off.

None of this will happen overnight. But among the progeny of *Ostpolitik* there may be a series of deals between Russia and major industries in West Germany, France and Italy which surpass anything they or Japanese counterparts have ever undertaken with her. In preliminary talks the British have not got far. But now even the United States has been negotiating contracts for which Russia would pay by high-level barter in kind – by tanker exports of natural gas, oil, timber or chrome when American reserves are being depleted. Yet this could be a reckless game. For the United States it would be rash because she might thus become dependent for supplies of energy on a Soviet rival. For the countries of Western Europe it would be still more imprudent if Russia could fix on them an impalpable grip of her own.

Arab oil States, to be sure, may be untrustworthy for other reasons. Yet much the same argument applies if there should be dependence on them by the West at a critical moment.

This analysis was published in Tokyo a year and a half before the Arabs adopted their boycott and oil exporters raised their prices, at the cost of developing as well as industrialised countries, so astronomically. One tragi-comic bit of the epilogue may be noted. After taking so much from Israel in expertise and economic assistance, African countries hopped aboard the pan-Arab bandwagon and in return were now offered the most paltry of rewards.

There have long been plans for Russia to pump natural gas through pipelines into Western Europe. These are not the same as a systematic Western effort to build her up technologically. Washington's justification for its turnabout may be that, as others will be doing the job anyhow, American industries cannot afford in an era of *Ostpolitik* and *détente* to abstain. Yet it is highly expedient for the Soviet Union thus to achieve relief in a variety of fields. As it is disencumbered there it can press all the harder against the West elsewhere – on the air, in the Middle East and upon the seven seas. A consolidation of the *status quo* between the Soviet *imperium* and non-Soviet Europe has made sense for many years. But if Russia outflanks Western Europe, those who strike self-deceptive bargains with her will have jeopardised more than themselves.

Never has the predicament of the West been so complex. Just as the United States has frowned hitherto upon whatever toughens the economic sinews of a Russian antagonist, so the enlargement of the European Community has been suspect in the Kremlin. But it, too, could change its mind if a Soviet outward thrust is to be accelerated. The West may relax when ritual Soviet diatribes against West German revanchism are no longer emitted. But, as West Europeans help modernise the Soviet economy, they might also give Moscow a chance for counter-penetration in their own policy-making sphere. Docile components of the European Community will have existing Soviet contracts to preserve – with the hope of more to come. What can be foreseen is a growing reluctance to offend an ostensible benefactor as disputes crop up over the affairs of the European Community or if anxiety mounts when the Soviet Union reaches out to more distant global theatres.

Ironies abound. There would have been no renovated German economy for Nazi warlords to pit against the West if British and American capitalism had not been politically so indiscriminate. The anticapitalist ideologues of the Kremlin may take a leaf from the same book. Nor is there the faintest sign that, as it is enlarged by the entry of Britain and other applicants, the European Community will do more collectively for its own defence. Some of its components may wonder instead whether, when the United States retrenches, they should not reinsure themselves with that very Soviet colossus which has rendered them insecure.

Not that that is what Herr Willy Brandt anticipated. *Ostpolitik,* as he conceived it, was to have NATO and American underpinnings. The sword he has forged, though, may be doubled-edged. What he did, so far as it denoted an acceptance of new postwar frontiers and did not embrace grandiose projects for the technological progress of the Soviet economy, had to be done; but he should not have tried to do it alone. And this was no local or regional blunder. The German problem should have figured in a wider settlement of the global contest between Russia and the West. Moscow took but did not give and may go on taking.

All in all, then, an analysis of deep-seated trends among major components hardly indicates that, as a bulwark of the West, an enlarged European Community will be more steadfast or rock-like. It might, as a free, dynamic economy outdo the Russian; it may not be as subservient as Finland. But, through an enlarged Community, Russia could get extra leverage. Hitherto she tried to procure this through the dissolution of blocs that her own Eurasian preponderance first called into existence. Even in trade agreements the Soviet Union harped upon bilateral negotiations between Comecon satellites and components of the European Community. But soon, if a politico-strategic twist can be imparted to the economics of *Ostpolitik,* Russia might sway an enlarged and unified Community from within. The neutralist, Third Force potential of that entity, while shattering the West, could still bother Moscow. Despite the fresh travail of the Czechs and Russian duplicity in the Middle East, it may do so no longer.

The risk is one which the Americans, eager for Western Europe to stand on its own feet, have always pooh-poohed. Rife for years was the comforting theory, sown by top Europeanisers among the British, that when the European Community is self-aggrandised the unity of the Western Alliance will be conserved intact. A drift from Atlantic moorings, if only because anti-American undercurrents are so potent, is more likely. In anything so unpredictable as the enlargement and unification of Western Europe there resides a hazard for the American mainstay of the West and for the West as a whole. Less would be imperilled, all the same, if Britain could still refrain.

What does impend, at any rate, is a reconstruction of the West and that is how the issue should have been debated. More recently the United States has detected that whatever enlarges the European Economic Community might enlarge the zone of trade discrimination. Still ignored, nevertheless, are cognate warnings that damage, in a politico-strategic perspective, may also be vast.

Washington has urged transatlantic allies to play the game in other respects. As recompense it could not deny them reiterated American support for the enlargement of the European Community.

It is a spectacle composed of paradox. Washington has been bracing itself to withstand an economic challenge from other huge agglomerations on strictly economic grounds. More than economics will be affected, however, if the United States puts across a new countervailing trade initiative. Only through centralising institutions can a semicontinental entity like the European Community rivet itself together. Cooperative but decentralised would be a project which, including other industrial countries, spans the oceans.

Meanwhile it was significant that, after August 1971, when means were discussed for healing the monetary rift between industrial countries of the free world, the United States suggested a package in which items negotiated at the outset will only be a foretaste of what is yet to come. American trade unions have perceived that, in an era of multinational corporations, classic free trade may simply export jobs. With compromises at home and abroad, however, Washington might still peg away for a trade liberalisation which lowers non-tariff as well as tariff barriers in both agricultural and industrial products.* Will other aggregations as economically outstanding as Japan and the European Community also be

*Earlier suggestions by the present writer for a countervailing American initiative as a substitute for the enlargement of the European Community through British entry were in tune with subsequent proposals by others for a wider free trade treaty. On this subject, The Atlantic Trade Study, London, published a pamphlet of his (July 1968) putting the case from a politico-strategic angle, and that became the writer's contribution to *New Trade Strategy for the World Economy*, ed. Prof. H. G. Johnson (Allen and Unwin Ltd, London, 1969; University of Toronto Press, Toronto and Buffalo, N.Y., 1969) pp. 77-163.

On the same topic a chapter by the present writer also appeared in *Destiny or Delusion?* ed. Douglas Evans (Victor Gollancz Ltd, London, 1971) pp. 185-207. Discussed, too, were hazards in overdoing *détente*.

prepared to make a fresh start? The American objective is to head off a more aggressive protectionism in the American Congress. A trade war will, after all, devastate beyond the confines of international trade.

It has been right for the United States to knock on such doors. But it is also through economic measures deprecated by Washington that the European Community will get the politico-strategic cohesion which Washington itself has promoted. On January 1, 1972, moreover, signatories carried out the last stage of tariff reductions under the Kennedy Round. And for the European Economic Community this also curtailed the advantages derived from the Common External Tariff behind a single tariff wall. What the Community still offered components was the Common Agricultural Policy. Nothing short of a drastic revision would satisfy British consumers or a critic like the United States.

And here an affirmative response from Japan may be crucial. It is from undue Americanisation of their economies that Canada, Britain and the countries of Western Europe have also shrunk. Reciprocal privileges, however, would be the multilateral nub of freer trade. Access to the American and Japanese home markets should compensate those who otherwise feel swamped.

Liberalised trade, besides, may bolster the comity of the West and in that, too, Japan can find politico-strategic merit. Whatever the European Community does, she would be as ill-served as any by a world economy partitioned throughout between semiclosed trading blocs. As one of the rich nations Japan cannot welcome an ever-deepening misery among the poor – their recoil from that free world on which its adversaries could batten. She herself is safe as long as the United States lives up to their defence pact and none flouts American global proficiency. It is these which, since the awesome traumas of World War II, have enabled Japan to concentrate on her own economic growth. But now, if Britain exchanges an oceanic for a continental role and thus enlarges the European Community, a lot might be transposed. So also, in her own corner of the earth, Japan herself could again destabilise. It was, after all, only at the end of World War II that Japan abandoned an ill-starred continental role – one which fanned out from the Chinese mainland and which, under altered circumstances, she might dream of resuming.

Nor should China, a former victim, have any valid complaint if instead the Japanese are thus drawn away from the mainland of East Asia. Danger on Soviet frontiers is what troubles her most. Southeast Asia could still obtain more Japanese aid for development and this may banish tenacious memories of Japanese conquest, prewar and wartime. But Tokyo would be wise to dodge rivalries that stretch beyond Sino-Soviet frontiers – far even from that Indian subcontinent where, with the break-up of Pakistan, they will fluctuate so kaleidoscopically. More rewarding for Japan, with new world-wide vistas, would be an extensive change of venue.

And it is for similar reasons that Siberian enterprise, with or without an American ally, may be counterproductive. Japan is worried over the vulnerability of her oil routes from the Persian Gulf as Russia expands at sea. She might only give one more hostage to fortune if she also becomes dependent on an oil pipeline across Soviet territory or on the supply of minerals and metals from the Soviet Union.

Japanese supplies from the Middle East and elsewhere pass through the Malacca Straits over which a controversy has flared about the ownership of what is the busiest of all maritime thoroughfares. Indonesia and Malaysia, backed by China, deny that these are international waters. The Soviet retort that they are such is consonant with the naval predominance Russia has attained in the Indo-Pacific theatre.

Capitalism, after all, is too serious a business for capitalists when they overlook politico-strategic realities and for politicians, Right, Left and Centre, when they do the same. Non-Soviet diplomacy may be inhibited by Soviet counter-penetration wherever there are massive deals with Russia. It would be as short-sighted for Tokyo, as it would be for Washington and the capitals of an enlarged European Community, to expedite the advance of Russian technology when curbs upon the arms race are chosen so disingenuously and when, to the Russian bid for Eurasian hegemony, there is so formidable an oceanic supplement.

A vision of *détente* hovers, nevertheless, over the West and, when the scales of power are global, East Asia, for weal or woe, will also feel the effect. Meanwhile the Soviet Union would gain most if an Egyptian client State, by clearing the Suez Canal, lets more Soviet war vessels pass from the Black Sea via the Mediterranean to the oil wells of the Persian Gulf and the sea lanes of the Indo-Pacific theatre. This, too, will intensify Russian surveillance of the Chinese coastline (apart from that mounted from Vladivostok) and of the heavy traffic to and from Japan. No less sweeping would be the Soviet watch of a reverse deployment offset by the American Seventh Fleet from the Western Pacific to the Middle East.

Against such expansion a countervailing initiative for liberalised trade may be dismissed as a foil that is blunt, fragile, even inappropriate. But whatever augments the unity and furthers the prosperity of the free world enhances its capacity to equip itself for the common defence. While the liberalisation of trade is an oblique exercise in this context, it is one that Japan, with courage on the home front and without violating politico-strategic taboos, could adopt. No open society is altruistic when it helps to magnify the vigour of other open societies or to keep their oceanic communications at work. But enlightened self-interest ordains that Japan belongs with them. And if Washington also clings to that principle, something constructive may yet be done.

In the end the main trading partners of the United States have no time to waste. When she combats protectionism abroad, she is combatting it at home and just as she negotiates under pressure so must they. But others can steel her to proceed whatever the European Community does. That entity reposes on an accord between French agriculture and German industry. France, backed by the Netherlands and others, will forbid any to modify the fundamentals of the Common Agricultural Policy or tamper with organs by which it is administered. When the American and French Presidents met in the Azores at the end of 1971, M. Pompidou seemed to bury a number of hatchets. On December 22, all the same, he still clutched one to wield against outsiders who condemned the farm policies of the European Community.

M. Pompidou did that by television interview. The only

sphere in which the Community had attained union, he contended, was agriculture. There will be no hope for economic and monetary union if this is undermined; for political union there will be even less. As a vague free trade area, he pointed out, Western Europe could not form a personality of its own. What, in other words, M. Pompidou had done was again to expose that innate conflict between the Gaullist French and quasi-Gaullists elsewhere who accept some features of full-blooded Gaullism while rejecting others.

Adamant was how her own President described the mood of France when he thus enunciated for the Community a Eurocentric character in perpetuity. West Germany, it is true, retorted that the Common Agricultural Policy will only flourish if it is preceded by economic and monetary union. But she is tugged hither and yon between the lures of *Ostpolitik* and the need for American military support. The French have their own brands of neutralism, some Gaullist and some leftwing, to purvey while, in their eyes, the Bonn Republic is, as a Trojan Horse for the United States, no more desirable than Britain.

Even in Britain, among proponents of the European Community, few demurred at utterances by the late Georges Pompidou on the subject of the Common Agricultural Policy. But under Harold Wilson, Prime Minister once more, and James Callaghan, as Foreign Secretary, a start was made on renegotiating the unsuitable terms their predecessors, Edward Heath and Sir Alec Douglas-Home, accepted for Britain's entry into the European Community.

Over the Common Agricultural Policy there may be room for administrative reforms but Community farmers were in no mood for these as profits melted away. West Germany did most, with Britain, to finance the scheme, and during the autumn of 1974 only agreed to higher farm prices after vetoing them. The French press raged. It saw that in Community affairs Bonn rather than Paris had become No. 1. As for the British people, the Community tried to win them over with a grant for cheaper sugar. British exports, though, were doing better elsewhere.

One plus for Britain is North Sea oil. As oil imports dwindle, so might the deficit in her balance of payments. She will have to liquidate foreign debts for outsize pipelines – the defences of the project being a domestic expenditure. And yet as long as Britain, like Norway, must share North Sea oil with others, she may not use it as much for socio-economic rehabilitation. If, however, she can persevere without Community membership, it is oceanic rather than continental affinities that this venture may ultimately renew.

Perhaps the formation of a bigger grouping, one devoted to liberalised trade, could still bring around France and her coadjutors. But first it must be formed. Can that be done if the European Community walks out? This is the question of questions, and if the answer is yes the United States and others must act before the rising tide of American protectionism engulfs them all.

The American goal is to liberalise trade between industrial countries of the free world while they do more and more for the less fortunate. It will be a setback if there are two of such groupings rather than one. Two will be better than three or four. Big or small, at any rate, the European Community should not rule the roost.

As for Britain, many of the British oppose having her join and thereby enlarge the European Community. The status quo, if she made the most of it, would be better for Britain than Europeanisation. Still better, though, would be the alternative that a multilateral treaty for liberalised trade could provide.

This might come too late. Yet some British opponents of Community membership may urge the withdrawal of their country even after the die is cast. Nor would Brussels be well advised, if there is still disaffection among the majority of the British people, to hold Britain to her bond. Then, too, while others may follow Britain into the European Community, fewer would depart in her wake. She can thus be diminished more than she can afterwards diminish it.

Britain's future is now obscure and nobody can tell what the consequences may be when the European Community exceeds what is its optimum size. The world contest is, besides, more intricate than ever; so, by the same token, is the preservation of the Atlantic nexus. Western Europe knows that it cannot dispense with the European role of the United States. It has been emboldened, nevertheless, to seek the means, through enlargement and unification, of separating itself from its own American guarantor. Those means may not always be employed as Community founding fathers have envisaged. The fact is that the European Community would not exist if a positive impulse did not lie behind it. The wider the repercussions of its enlargement, though, the more negative they become. The free world does not yet realise that Eurocentric and global reckonings are hard to reconcile with each other. The sooner it does so the better off it will be.

15 EEC as a Third Force: Tryouts over the Middle East*

Many strands in global politics were crossed when, with the October War of 1973, Arabs and Israelis waged their fourth round since 1948. A crisis on the rim of the West brought one to pass within it. But this had long been germinating.

Israel may have been taken by surprise when Arab States attacked her on the Day of Atonement, October 6, 1973, but in their behaviour, pro and con, other Powers ran true to form. A month later a formal declaration even lined up the European Economic Community (or Common Market) with the enemies of that beleaguered land. There was, though, nothing new about this. Community members had been attempting for years to co-ordinate foreign policies and it was at the expense of Israel that, from the outset, the EEC tried to do so.

Such an assertion will meet with disbelief. There has been publicity about disputes between the EEC and various segments of the free world over trade and monetary affairs; on both sides of the Atlantic, however, major opinion media had always soft-pedalled other adverse Community trends. Then, too, at one juncture Israel might have joined a free trade area which, despite protests from Washington, the EEC was devising for Mediterranean non-members. A need to conserve the flow of oil from Arab producers is now given as the sole excuse for an anti-Israeli stance. The fact is, nevertheless, that Israel was the butt of hostile manifestations by the European Economic Community more than two years before the oil imbroglio came to a head. To these the Netherlands subscribed reluctantly in the autumn of 1973. But the pro-Arab sympathies of the European Community had been apparent long before Arab countries brandished the oil weapon as a

*This essay was first published as an article, 'Ganging up against Israel', in the *Spectator* (London, 12 Jan 1974).

means of cowing the West and of getting the United States, by a circuitous method, to forsake Israel.

Western Europe is rich again and it wants to have a commensurate say in world politics. Not that Humpty Dumpty, after so great a fall, expects again to be, as he once was, the pivot of world politics. American and Russian superpowers now hold the scales. As an ensemble however, the European Economic Community would like to deal with other giant aggregations – the American, the Russian, the Chinese, the Japanese – as an equal. The question is, though, whether the EEC is prepared to speak abroad with a resonant single voice. It has not yet built up the sort of unified statehood through which other titans express themselves. It is, moreover, unequipped for making a contribution to the maintenance of a wider free world order or even to preserve, under the North Atlantic Alliance, a due share of its own semi-continental ramparts against the Warsaw Pact. For many years American policymakers made light of any who pointed to the neutralist, anti-American Third Force predispositions that lurked in the European Community. These, nevertheless, burst forth during the Arab-Israeli war of October 1973. Only Portugal, among Atlantic allies of the United States, granted the use of facilities (in the Azores) to American aircraft when they flew to Israel with essential war supplies.

Rumour has it that Madrid, though pro-Arab, allowed the American air base at Torrejon also to be used for midair refuelling of American replacements being flown to Israel. The United States has her own pact with Franco's Spain which, as a country governed by a relic of Fascist-Nazi days, is excluded from the North Atlantic Alliance.

But it is a toss-up whether even Portugal, having overthrown her Right-wing dictatorship, would reply as favourably again to a similar American request. The privileges enjoyed under lease by the United States at Lajes, a Portuguese air base in the Azores lying midway between North America and the Middle East, are highly unpopular. Portugal was denied Arab oil, moreover, after the previous regime, with much otherwise so repugnant, enabled the American airlift to proceed. General Costa Gomes supplanted General

Spinola as President and his government bent more towards the Left. Staying in NATO, they were susceptible to neutralism. It was with them that Washington had to arrange further access to a key American base in the Azores.

Meanwhile it had taken eight days for the airlift to start and for the delay various explanations have been offered. One school attributed it to James Schlesinger, the Defence Secretary. Another suggested that until President Nixon himself set the airlift going it was Henry Kissinger who as Secretary of State still ran everything.

A number of motives have been ascribed for a gamble on the fate of Israel. Fresh supplies were needed before she could push Egyptian troops back across the Suez Canal. If this did not happen Cairo might feel less humiliated in negotiating with Jerusalem. If, too, an oil boycott had been surmised, less offence should be given Arab progenitors. Russo-American co-operation in the Middle East was, it was as supposed, also desired – scant as that had been.

None of this worked out. After a bad week for Israel the United States no longer withheld supplies. Towards both, however, Washington's chief transatlantic allies were unhelpful throughout. Apologists may seek to justify them by comparing their sloth with American procrastination. They should look again.

It is, to be sure, Western Europe and not the Middle East that is covered by the North Atlantic Alliance. Strategically, as had been revealed by the Afro-Asian campaigns of the two world wars and the postwar Truman Doctrine, the defence of the one region is mixed up with the defence of the other.

Soon, however, fighting in the Middle East was again halted and West European chancellories argued that, for peace-making, they, with the two superpowers, possessed a unique prerogative. But Russia is suspect and Israel would have felt abandoned if even Britain and France planted themselves, under one guise or another, on the scene of combat. In the United Nations, at any rate, the United States objected to peacekeeping contingents from those who enjoyed permanent seats on the Security Council – the United States herself, the Soviet Union, Britain and France, with China abstaining from the vote. And when Russia threatened anyhow to go ahead on her own, an American precautionary alert (with 'Hands off' as its grim nuclear message) indicated that the United States was not bluffing.

Moscow climbed down. It scored, nevertheless, when the oil embargoes it had long proposed to Arab oil countries were adopted. For the nonce, on the other hand, the American precautionary alert had saved the independence of Israel from a Soviet stranglehold – even though defensible frontiers, life-savers in 1973, may subsequently be narrowed under post-bellum pressure from Washington. And the European Community, having cold-shouldered its American guarantor, opened a rift in the Atlantic Alliance over which the Kremlin will have shed no tears.

The dilemma is one, moreover, that a federal union for the European Community cannot, as many now imagine, do anything to resolve. It was clear before the autumn of 1973 that such a vehicle would only accentuate impulses that are neutralist, anti-American and Third force in effect. Yet these can be diminished. The European Community might, after all, be premature in throwing its weight about. Britain is a new member and the British people do not like what awaits them within that body. Terms of entry may be renegotiated. But will renegotiation bear fruit? If this gets nowhere Britain might withdraw from the EEC. A regional entity, commanding fewer resources and exerting less influence, may be the result.

What, at any rate, must be remembered about the Community's anti-Israel posture is that there had been signs of trouble for several years before the Arab-Israeli war of October 1973 and these must not be neglected if the situation is to be seen in perspective. Events have moved so fast that it will have been forgotten how Japanese militants recruited by Palestinian terrorists mowed down at Lod, the Israeli international airport, eleven Puerto Rican pilgrims, seven citizens of Israel and five other innocent travellers.* The Security Council of the United Nations, glossing as always over pan-Arab misdeeds, railed once more at Israel for

*The Israeli international airport has been renamed after the late statesman David Ben Gurion.

having mounted reprisals at the Lebanese bases of Palestinian terrorists. Unabashed, too, was the spirit of cynicism in which members of the EEC nodded assent.

Three months later the same West European combine staged a repeat performance. During September, after Israeli athletes were assassinated at the Munich Olympiad, Israeli aircraft struck once more at the Syrian and Lebanese havens of Arab terrorists. Russian and Chinese vetoes sheltered the latter, with their hosts and sponsoring governments, from condemnation by the Security Council. But for a subsequent American veto Israel would have borne the entire blame. And so, among others, the Community bloc, with the Pompidou regime in the van, mocked simple equity – and Britain under Edward Heath did the same.

Nor was the Security Council the only organ of the United Nations that, during 1972, put Israel in the dock. The General Assembly, before the adjournment of its annual autumn meeting, passed a resolution, 86 to 7, condemning the Israelis for annexationist procedures in the occupied territories. The Community group – Britain, France, Belgium, Italy and Luxembourg – had persuaded Egypt and her coadjutors to eliminate from their resolution a threat of sanctions against Israel, but this, under the United Nations Charter, the General Assembly could not, in any case, have enforced. The text, nevertheless, was still more pro-Arab and anti-Israel than any similar statement by the General Assembly hitherto. In voting for it the countries of Western Europe were arrayed with the Soviet Union, patron of Egypt, Syria and Iraq. The United States, with China, was numbered among the thirty-one that abstained.

Then, during April 1973, Israeli commandos killed three Arab terrorist leaders in the heart of Beirut and the United Nations Security Council rebuked Israel for the daring reprisal she had undertaken. An Anglo-French resolution was less one-sided, though, than its predecessor and here, too, the United States did no more than abstain. On July 26, the United States cast another veto. The Security Council had been making a broad survey of the Arab-Israeli conflict and might have passed a resolution which, as usual, censured Israel alone. Against her Britain and France ganged up with

Russia once more. And in August 1973 it was the prospect of another American veto which eliminated a threat of sanctions when the Security Council admonished Israel for intercepting an Arab airliner in Lebanese airspace and searching it on Israeli soil.

Unison between Paris and London against Jerusalem involved Washington. In the North Atlantic Alliance, however, no deeper breach yawned until the Arab-Israeli war of October 1973. But when the EEC issued its pro-Arab statement in Brussels on November 6, this had not only been preceded by numerous try-outs in the two organs of the United Nations. Account must be taken of a still earlier episode, one divulged early in the winter of 1972. During the previous year a series of unusual conversations had been held at Luxembourg between members and would-be members of the European Community.

'The talks have been shrouded in secrecy,' it was reported by *The Times* (February 4, 1972). 'This is no doubt in part a reaction to the damage done by leaks last spring when the Six drafted a secret memorandum on the Middle East – their first joint foreign policy venture. The Israelis considered it to be too pro-Arab, accused the Germans of caving in to the French and vented their disappointment on Herr Walter Scheel, the West German Foreign Minister, when he visited Israel.'

Dismay in Jerusalem was natural enough as the French and West Germans broke ground and, with other components, explored how, within the European Community, they might concur over world affairs. The French, West Germans and British are the prime components of the European Community. Each had pro-Arab leanings. Anti-Israel was the mood in which it all started.

The Community has done most in the West to stir things up against Israel, and France has done most to stir things up in the Community. About her motives there is no mystery. In a number of Arab countries – Syria, Lebanon, Tunisia, Algeria and Morocco – French banks, oil companies and commercial houses have long held sway; and as French economic imperialism thrives behind a nationalist, anti-colonial facade, it panders to pan-Arab feelings. Not that middle-rank officials or the French people as a whole nurse the anti-Israel sentiments that the upper echelons display. Nor has France always taken the same path. Bold zigzags mark her course towards NATO and towards entry by Britain into the European Community. She has not always been against Israel. *Sacro egoismo,* Gaullist style, was ostensibly what induced her during the Six-day War of 1967 to reverse herself.

Before his retirement, General de Gaulle's taunt over the 'domineering' qualities of Jews revealed the degree to which the anti-Dreyfus credo that was rife during his boyhood outlasted his struggle with Hitler – a German whose anti-Semitic furies consumed many of de Gaulle's own compatriots, famous and obscure alike, with Jewish antecedents. As for the General's political heir, Pompidou, he had not only kept out of the French Resistance but exercised his right as President to pardon a Frenchman who collaborated with the Nazis during their occupation of France.

One gauge of Gaullist aims in this context has been downright bad faith over the sale of arms. The United States substituted her Phantoms for the French Mirage aircraft which Israel had bought and paid for but of which she could not obtain delivery. So too, there was a dispute between Paris and Jerusalem over missile-firing French patrol ships purchased by the Israelis and for which, nevertheless, an escape from St Nazaire was contrived. Under President Pompidou, moreover, France had supplied Libya with Mirage jets, although with the pledge that Egypt would not use them against Israelis. Egyptians, however, were trained to pilot these and some of them were shot down during the Arab-Israeli war of 1973 by Israel. There was also a significant incident at Djibouti where the French forbade an American destroyer to leave port and go to the help of a blockaded American freighter.

Then The Hague offended the Arabs by endorsing Community strictures of Israel and yet staying pro-Israel. The French, with the British, thereupon baulked at sharing oil with the Dutch. This was scarcely a boost for the idea of a co-ordinated foreign policy by the Nine. Yet in the National Assembly only the Communist Party lent M. Pompidou unanimous support and everywhere French diplomacy flouted what, by the findings of opinion polls, was the will of the nation.

But the cruellest recent blows to emanate from Western Europe were West German in origin. Israeli athletes and trainers did not only die because of blunders by authorities of the Bonn Republic at the Munich Olympiad of September 1972; within seven weeks the rest of the Arab terrorists were released. And yet with Arab affairs Germans have had little to do since the first world war, except for a brief second world war interlude under Rommel. They were plunged into these, however, with the rise of Israel – a land to which a surviving remnant of European Jewry fled and where the Bonn Republic, ashamed and repentant over incalculable evil wrought in the German name, acquired a moral outpost. But even before the Munich Olympiad, with its grim sequel, the process of reconciliation between Israel and West Germany had been more erratic than is realised.

During 1971, for example, when the Six drafted their first secret memorandum on the Middle East, the aftermath suggested that the West Germans saw eye to eye with the French and were already letting the Israelis down.

What Israel wanted from the Bonn Republic was that it would always take up the cudgels for her. As compared with the Nazi affiliations of his predecessor, Dr Kurt Kiesinger, there was Herr Willy Brandt's own valiant anti-Nazi record and the unparalleled gesture of the West German Chancellor when he knelt at the Warsaw ghetto memorial. Nazi atrocities had produced a special relationship between Bonn and Jerusalem. West Germany differed, besides, from her European allies over one point with no precedent: a stipulation by the vanquished that a victor must undertake to evacuate occupied territory before a peace settlement had been signed. Yet Ostpolitik, as a rapprochement between West Germany and the Soviet imperium, engendered a rapprochement between West Germany and clients of Russia among the Arabs. How special, under these circumstances, was Israel's special relationship with the Bonn Republic likely to be?

Henceforth, as between Arabs and Israelis, West Germany played no favourites. The West German recognition of Israel seven years before had prompted Arab States to cut ties with Bonn. These, with a Soviet mentor blowing hot and cold, were restored. When the European Community groomed itself for its debut as a major factor in world politics, a pro-Arab bias emerged at once. It was Herr Brandt himself, furthermore, who, a week before the Arab League acted upon overtures from West Germany, proposed a second Community effort – nothing less than mediation in the Middle East.

By June 8, 1972, Egypt and the Bonn Republic were officially in touch with each other again. Diplomatists intimated that the Egyptian Government and other states of the Arab League had been pleased by Herr Brandt's attempt to conduct an impartial policy in the Middle East. But the rumble of conflict was what the Middle East first brought to West Germany. In September Cairo rejected an appeal for co-operation from Herr Brandt at the Munich Olympiad before Arab kidnappers, after killing two Israelis, slaughtered the rest of their victims. Yet a wrangle that supervened did not last long. Despite the backing that terrorist bands procured from most Arab States, Bonn hastily absolved the latter from complicity in what had happened.

West Germany, as far as Israel was concerned, had found the road back with no difficulty. More awkward was her later quest in Arab-Israeli affairs for the middle of the road.

Salt was poured on raw wounds when, during October 1972, Bonn surrendered Arab gunmen, imprisoned since their crimes at the Olympic games in September, to hijacking liberators. West Germany had been making amends to Israel since the days of Konrad Adenauer. Yet even Herr Willy Brandt now vacillated. Jerusalem must have banked on Bonn's willingness to follow through. As it falters, there are no champions among the main components of the Community on whom Jerusalem may count.

It was a noteworthy hour, all the same, when, in June 1973, the West German Chancellor, unlike other foreign Heads of Government, went to Israel. If he exhibited moral courage, so did Mrs Meir, then Israeli Prime Minister, when she received a West German Chancellor on the soil of the Jewish State and accepted his invitation to pay West Germany a return visit.

Ambivalence, however, is what still typifies the attitude of the Bonn Republic towards Israel and, since the Arab-Israeli war of October 1973, has done so as much as ever. Unlike other Community allies, West Germany first permitted but then forbade the United States to fly war supplies out of her German depots for the succour of Israeli fighting services. Two Israeli ships also loaded up at Bremenshaven; the third, hoisting the Star of David, was stopped lest Arabs take it amiss. Oil for the Bonn Republic is refined at Rotterdam and Arab States notified West Germany that, with a pro-Israel public in the Netherlands, there must be no show of solidarity with her.

In the Upper and Lower House, Herr Brandt endeavoured (November 13, 1973) to rectify moral damage by restating the reasons for a special relationship with Israel. He also commended the Community pronouncement (Brussels, November 6) which overweighted against Israel the more balanced United Nations resolution of 1967. Confusion persists.

Nor are such fluctuations apt to abate. The two Germanies have joined the United Nations but while they belong to competing global camps the problem of Israel is not likely to set them apart. After the first world war the German people rebelled against the stigma of war guilt. After the second world war it was guilt of another kind that elicited West German reparations for Israel and indemnities for such German-Jewish victims as were left. East Germany, as Moscow's principal European client, long carped at any such obligation. But all of this stems from a past that the younger generation of Germans, East and West, never knew.

Time, moreover, has also been working to Israel's detriment in world politics generally. Remorse after German infamy derived from the Christian conscience. There are few signs of this today in most of the European Community or at the United Nations. In the world body Afro-Asians call the tune and, with the Soviet bloc, Moslem States have been quick to exploit their opportunity. During the 1940s the immeasurably macabre statistics of Nazi iniquity were still fresh when the United Nations General Assembly authorised the creation of a Jewish state and admitted it to membership. In the 1970s no similar proceeding would be remotely conceivable.

Then there is Britain, a neophyte among major Community policy-makers, but one who prior to the independence of Israel had had with her the closest of associations. It was to create a Jewish National Home that she had been assigned a Mandate for Palestine by the League of Nations while derelict Turkish lands, infinitely more vast in extent, were carved out for Arab desert chieftains. London, though, had whittled down space for the Jewish Homeland before Nazi persecutions enhanced its value.

After the war of 1967, Israel would have negotiated with Arab neighbours under Security Council Resolution No. 242 as sponsored at the United Nations by the Wilson government. For the Heath government, however, a less equitable version was offered in a speech at Harrogate during November 1970 by Sir Alec Douglas-Home. Even more extreme, after the Arab-Israeli war of 1973, were the pro-Arab dicta of the Community which at Brussels (November 6) the British, with the French, did most to formulate.

No doubt Sir Alec Douglas-Home recognised Israel's right to existence. A rush to the rescue after she had succumbed would, all the same, not be worth much. The United States herself, moreover, had long been urging Europeanisation upon Britain and this was now put to the test of battle. In commercial morality London emulated Paris when it banned the export of ammunition and spare parts for Centurion tanks that Israel had bought from Britain. The Heath government did further harm when it forbade the passage to Israel via Cyprus of American war supplies and ferried fighter bombers.

From a time-table of the American precautionary alert, it may be gathered that in October 1973 Washington informed London of what it contemplated first of all and other European allies as soon as possible. But while this could have been treated as a courtesy, with historic Anglo-American undertones, it no longer impressed Downing Street. Paramount at Westminster then was a European commitment.

Next came a furore between the United States and the European Community as a whole when there had to be co-operation by the West for parrying Arab oil blackmail. During the first half of 1974, however, new Ministers took office in Britain, France and West Germany. As President of France there was now M. Valery Giscard d'Estaing with M. Jacques Chirac as Prime Minister and, as Foreign Minister, M. Jean Sauvagnargues. In the Bonn Republic Herr Walter Scheel stepped up to a Presidency that did not, as among the French, run the show; that duty fell to the Chancellor who was now Herr Helmut Schmidt – with Herr Hans-Dietrich Genscher as Foreign Minister. In Britain, meanwhile, they had all been preceded by Mr Harold Wilson for another tour as Prime Minister with Mr James Callaghan as Foreign Secretary.

Among representative democracies, however, Heads of Government, as distinguished from Heads of State, may not hold office very long. For the moment, though, British policy over the Middle East and over Community membership was no longer being made in Paris, while even at the Elysée Palace and on the Quai d'Orsay the rabid anti-Americanism of two Gaullist Presidencies seemed momentarily to subside.

A period of less irrational Europeanism will not console Jerusalem, all the same, if, towards the Israelis, Washington should ever waver. Israel was bewildered again when the United States voted to condemn her for retaliating after Arab terrorist murders in the frontier village of Kiryat Shemona went typically unrebuked by the UN Security Council. Washington probably expected that this, like the sale of American arms to fire-breathing Arab States, would accelerate disengagement as mediated by Secretary Kissinger after the October war. When, nevertheless, Arab terrorists massacred Israeli schoolchildren at Maalot, killed settlers at Kibbutz Shamir and others at Nahariya, even the United Nations Security Council lapsed for once into silence.

Then, among American assurances given Damascus and Jerusalem, one particularly has not held up. This was a pledge that in diplomacy the United States would take the Israeli side if pan-Arab terrorists extorted reprisals once more. There are also to be American reconnaissance flights for monitoring Egyptian, Syrian and Israeli disengagement zones.

In June 1974 when President Nixon conferred with Israelis as well as Arabs on his trip to the Middle East, he denounced pan-Arab terrorism and reaffirmed the right of the Israelis to 'secure borders'. As for increased American economic assistance to Israel, this could now be subject to long-range planning. But with the political volatility of their Arab neighbours in mind, Israelis would have been less worried if there had been no grant of American nuclear assistance so as to match the American grant of nuclear reactors to Egypt. And yet Israel rather than Egypt, with her pan-Arab oil connections and her capacity for harnessing the flow of water over the Aswan Dam, is the one that needs fresh sources of energy.

It is, though, life among both of the superpowers that still keeps Israel guessing. If the European allies of the United States do not soon make good ensuing deficiencies, a reduction in the number of American troops stationed across the Atlantic could invite Russian ascendancy beyond the Soviet imperium. The defence of non-Soviet Europe has, besides, its maritime as well as its territorial phase. When long-range weapons are also sea-based, the land and sea frontiers of Western Europe stand or fall together.

And in this regard the southern littoral of Western Europe has ports that must always welcome ships of the American Sixth Fleet – with those of its allies. They may not do this, however, if, bowing to Soviet predominance, Popular Fronts take over; if the French or Italian Left arrange matters with Moscow; if, in the European Community, anti-American Third Force neutralism, which Gaullism itself promoted, gets the upper hand. American warships may or may not be older than those that Russia employs. But what the Israelis could fear are the onerous conditions the Kremlin might impose if, lest the Mediterranean becomes a trap, the American Sixth Fleet should ever be recalled and Israel is encircled.

With this problem, moreover, the future of the Balkans, that historic trouble-spot, may be coupled. Via Hungary or Bulgaria (if the latter joins the Soviet Union and there is a Russian corridor through Roumania), the Soviet Union could get direct access to Yugoslavia, after all – when, that is, Tito has gone and nobody can bend the chief antagonistic Yugoslav sub-nationalities, the Croats, Serbs and Slovenes, to his will. The outcome might be an outlet for Russia on the

Adriatic – another one of those warm-water ports she has always craved. Next door to Italy, a Mediterranean signatory of the North Atlantic Alliance, the Soviet Union could thus acquire an Adriatic-Mediterranean naval base of its own.

When, all the same, Greece returned unexpectedly to civilian rule in 1974 the position of the North Atlantic Alliance should have been ameliorated. For the American Sixth Fleet that country had long been a key Mediterranean outpost. But after the undeclared war on Cyprus, Greece chartered a less NATO-oriented course.

At the eastern end of the Mediterranean, as a matter of fact, Haifa (apart from Turkish ports) might soon have become the only safe haven for the American Sixth Fleet. Israel, however, lies beyond the Turkish borders of the Atlantic Alliance and has a neutral status – a posture not likely to be altered when the West has Arab States to woo.

Russian war vessels, moreover, may not always be debarred, in spite of an American-Egyptian rapprochement, from Egyptian ports, and Latakia in Syria is still at their disposal. Then, too, as patron of Iraq, the Soviet Union is well poised for regional hegemony. Iran, for one, may be caught in a vise. From Iraq, anyhow, Russia can sit on land at the head of the Persian Gulf, with all its oil riches, while she may also reach its foot by sea.

Illuminating the triumph of history over geography, Israel has had a position on the map which, paradoxically, is both an asset and a liability. For the bulk of her sea traffic the best route is the one between southern Europe and northern Africa. More of a gamble for Israel since the war of October 1973 is transit between her various ports and the Orient. Even if Israeli shipping ever proceeds through the Suez Canal, Egypt has always been allowed to evade its rules with impunity. And today Israel cannot reckon as safely as she has with the Aqaba route to so vital a southern gateway as Elath. She does not relax her grip on the Sharm el Sheikh – Sinai locale in 1967 for a brazen violation of guarantees, Egyptian and American, in which the United Nations acquiesced. Nowadays, however, it is at the mouth of the Red Sea that traffic to and from Israel may also be menaced – if, that is, the Straits of Bab-el-Mandeb pass under pan-Arab control.

What, on the other hand, the Red Sea artery does afford is quicker naval access to Indo-Pacific waters – from the Soviet naval base at Odessa and from the Mediterranean ports of the West. If the Suez Canal is unblocked and detente falls short of a full world settlement, the United States and Russia will vie unceasingly for the oil riches of the Persian Gulf. Here, as in the Mediterranean and beyond, global counteracting power can maintain freedom of the seas. And if it does maritime communications through Elath, as through Haifa and Ashdod, may be renewed.

The Middle East, however, is a zone in which Western Europe desires to intervene again but where, as it has now demonstrated, it will only make mischief for the West as well as Israel. On home fronts it must get its priorities straight first of all. Abroad the EEC should recollect that it itself once favoured those 'secure and recognised boundaries' which figure as much as 'withdrawal' for Israel in Resolution No. 242 of the United Nations Security Council. And less self-righteous, too, might have been the European Community when, on November 6, 1973 it borrowed the phrase against 'the inadmissibility of the acquisition of territory by force'. Which among the West Europeans has been applying that axiom to the Soviet Union with its swollen post-Yalta frontiers and as it jumps from the Middle East to the Indo-Pacific theatre? When, too, was strict territorial rectitude invoked against Transjordan for tearing up the UN Partition Plan in 1948 and seizing, with the West Bank, East Jerusalem?

Israel preferred to cede much of the Left Bank to Jordan but not for a Palestinian State – a radical one that could look to Moscow. Nor will unrest in Jordan leave Saudi Arabia unaffected. Oil-rich Arab regimes may even ruin the economy of the West. There might be little protection against them. Against subversion by rivals of the West, can they protect themselves?

As for the EEC, its components should have learned from the years of appeasement that when its pusillanimity is a danger to others it will be a danger to itself. Today, with all its pride in the civilised society it inherited, it defers to peoples as backward as the Arabs; and the Soviet Union, pushing far afield, must perceive that West European compliance with a crack from the Russian knout may be even more servile. The European Community could not enforce its attempt (November 6, 1973) to cosset Arab states by redrafting UN Security Council Resolution No. 242. It should also have known how, above all, Article 51 of the United Nations Charter revalidates for Israel the right of self-defence. The security of that small land presupposes that, in upholding world order, the West will prevail. So does that of the European Community. And that the West itself should be riven over Israel's struggle for existence is, among ironies of history, far from trivial.

PART SIX

Concluding Reflections

16 Topsy-Turvy as a Principle of Statecraft

With an updated running commentary, this book has attempted to show how some great issues looked at crucial turning-points during the middle years of the twentieth century. But now, as so often before, the West has fundamentals to scan afresh. And it must not so mistake current trends that, while trying to make things better for itself, it only makes them worse. Nor are the merits and demerits of such an argument as obvious or as unequivocal as might be surmised. They form therefore the underlying theme – in an analysis written for this book – of one's concluding reflections.

I

The West should have learned from the 1930s that change is not always for the better but the lesson is growing dim. New elements of power may emerge. Much could be realigned ideologically. As power and ideology interact, there is no assurance that the West will come out on top. It cannot flourish tomorrow unless it ponders the consequences of what it does or leaves undone today.

Such have been the risks of nuclear warfare that a *détente* could not be long delayed. An all-out settlement between East and West is harder to envisage. Within the West itself, moreover, a redistribution of power began prior to the East-West *détente.* And the one process affects the other. Always to be remembered on both sides of the Atlantic is that when statecraft flouts experience it might only turn itself upside down.

If major antagonists dare not fight each other, they must coexist. It is assumed that competition between them will henceforth be on a higher ideological plane. But if there are one-sided arrangements to accompany a *détente,* the West may still be caught short.

Since the test ban and the anti-proliferation agreement, the United States has signed a treaty with Russia to subdue the arms race in nuclear defensive weapons (Salt I). Another treaty to stop it in nuclear offensive weapons (Salt II) is being debated – less auspiciously. Measures may thus be taken to forestall an irreparable holocaust. Moscow, nevertheless, is now afraid that the United States and China will band together. Apart from that, however, the Soviet Union has not only sought nuclear parity with the United States but is pushing on towards nuclear supremacy. It has also been outbuilding the North Atlantic Alliance in the domain of conventional weapons. Between Russia and the Western camp, as a matter of fact, there might be no military showdown of any kind. And yet it may be that even for a broad settlement across the board, the Soviet Union will have accumulated more numerous bargaining counters than the West.

Nor is this all that protracts the global contest. There is the difference between rival systems. Democracy at its worst is still rooted in popular consent, in live-and-let-live. Dictatorship would be overthrown from within if it did not rule by force. More than once free societies have been too easy-going. Tension at home and abroad is what gives dictatorship, Left or Right, much of its impetus.

Never has the conflict of political systems been so widespread. And there has always been the prospect that *détente* may alter means rather than ends. During the cold war, democracies might have overstated their case. To understate it would have been even more topsy-turvy. It is, after all, through ideology that nations and groups of nations make their purpose known; that they tell what it will be like wherever their writ runs. For the sake of *détente,* the United States and her allies have cut across ideological barriers. How far they can go remains to be seen.

A newer American realism not only adapts that of Truman and Acheson to altered circumstances but is itself accompanied by a dash of paradox. Some commentators have imagined that as mentors, with policies shorn of ideological links, the United States could borrow from nineteenth century European Ministers like Metternich of Austria and

Bismarck of Prussia. The local power of such autocrats was steeped, though, in a most discredited brand of ideology. After the defeat of Napoleon and the Congress of Vienna had met, the British Foreign Secretary became, with the Tsar Alexander I and Prince Metternich, a pillar of the Holy Alliance. 'A piece of sublime mysticism and nonsense' was, nevertheless, how Castlereagh himself soon ridiculed that archaic triumvirate.

It was by the oppression of subject nationalities that the Austrian Minister kept the Hapsburg domains together. It was, too, by the seizure of Alsace-Lorraine that, some years later, the Prussian Chancellor laid foundations for that reversal of alliances which also became a major cause of World War I.

Worthier of study was realism without *Realpolitik* – the manner in which, from the days of Phillip of Spain to those of the Emperor William II, the British preserved their independence by upholding the European balance of power. Before primacy in the West moved across the Atlantic, Britain derived strength from overseas affinities while she could only maintain these by ensuring her security across the English Channel. What the young American Republic owed to British maritime pre-eminence was acknowledged by Thomas Jefferson and James Monroe: to its debt witness was borne subsequently by Captain Mahan, Admiral Dewey and John Hay. During the Spanish American War of 1898, the other Great Powers would have rammed themselves between the two belligerents if the Royal Navy had not held the ring for the United States.

Soon Anglo-American disputes were to be either liquidated or soft-pedalled. And in world politics an Anglo-American factor thus made its bow. Against the German naval challenge, when Britain had to bring warships back to home waters, she could now leave her interests in the Western Hemisphere to the care of a renovated American Navy. Without the Anglo-American factor Theodore Roosevelt, as go-between during the Russo-Japanese War (1904-5) might not have got far. But after World War I, the United States reverted to a strict non–interventionism. Yet World War II and its East-West sequel were to make evident how the

Anglo-American factor had endured – if only to become the resilient core of a power structure for the West as a whole.

What dimmed this epoch-making feat, at once so lengthy, so disjointed and with so many caveats, was the rise and fall of Woodrow Wilson. During the second half of World War I the United States assisted Britain and France in restoring a European balance which President Wilson himself had decried. He was unable, however, to extract from the Senate that two-thirds vote by which the 1919 settlement had to be ratified. If the Covenant of the League of Nations had been accepted, it would have required the United States to join, under Article X, in rectifying everywhere breaches of the territorial *status quo.* But when this clause was thrown out, the Senate also shelved a specific Anglo-American treaty of guarantee to France – one by which the European balance of power might have been preserved, the demoralisation of the British and French between the wars staved off and World War II averted. In that new struggle Winston Churchill, Josef Stalin and Franklin Roosevelt were to be the architects of victory. While Churchill did not invent the Anglo-American factor he revivified it and, in his own double-tongued fashion, the second President Roosevelt trailed behind.

The North Atlantic Alliance took shape under President Harry Truman. It would not have been needed, though, if the free world could have relied on the United Nations as a vehicle of security for the West. The essence of that which France was denied in 1920 had, nevertheless, been proffered her and her neighbours at last – though with NATO, the operational agent of the North Atlantic Alliance, France herself has played fast and loose.

The resumption of power politics was preceded, all the same, by a brief wartime *détente* between Russia and the West. So, too, lest they wipe each other out, a truce had once been patched up between Christian and Turk, Protestant and Catholic. Only an overriding threat could, for an expedient interval, bring together enemies of Nazi Germany who were themselves ideologically so diverse. Less than two years after the Nazi-Soviet Pact had precipitated World War II, the Nazis assailed their Communist co-signatories; but, while Russia and the West preserved their own ill-assorted systems in unison, they fell apart once victory had been clinched. From the defence of Berlin and Southern Korea to the Cuban missile crisis and the enunciation of the Brezhnev Doctrine, from war in Vietnam and Southern Asia to that in the Middle East, rival camps have kept an eye on each other. *Détente* suggests, however, that they will pull their punches if both have the same nuclear peril to dispel. A European conclave has accordingly tried to determine the contacts that may be feasible between the two sides of the Iron Curtain. Matters are further complicated, though, by the Sino-Soviet feud.

Seemingly, through agreement with the Bonn Republic and *détente* with the West, Russia can pay more attention to China. But, while the West lags in strategic preparedness, it can give Russia pause through diplomacy. By her own parallel, even-handed *détente* with the Chinese, the United States may be indicating that their country will not be abandoned or East Asia excluded from any complex new equilibrium. And if that is so, the United States, by bolstering up the weaker against the stronger, will have been doing globally what Britain had long done nearby to maintain the European balance of power.

Something less precarious, though, is what the United States now seeks. It would be 'a stable structure, not a classical balance of power', explained President Nixon when he reported to the Congress on foreign policy in May 1973. Yet absolute stability is an unattainable goal until rival camps pursue the same objective and when, against an ideology based on war without conflict, the implements of war must still be amassed. There can be no substitute for a power balance until all major contestants join in the search for one. Such a day is still far off.

What the United States may do is stop ideological competition at the front door and let it in at the back. The American concept of peace rests (as Secretary Kissinger informed the United Nations General Assembly on 24 September 1973) 'not merely on a balance of force but on shared aspirations'. And yet, apart from co-existence itself, what shared aspirations are rival camps likely to breed? It may take more than international trade or scientific and technological collaboration to revamp the chief adversaries of free societies. There is much in the West that the ill-intentioned can exploit against it.

Not that a classical balance of power has persisted. What banished it was the West's own monumental folly between world wars. Two antagonistic superpowers, a Eurasian and a North American, have ruled the roost since World War II; the age, furthermore, is one also of intercontinental weaponry. The upshot could, literally or metaphorically, shake the earth. The old European balance of power was supplanted by a new global balance and, for free societies, a more extensive power structure has been ordained.

In contention between Russia and the West, nevertheless, Western Europe still serves as a decisive makeweight. Such are its human resources, advanced productive capacity and key strategic position that, by wresting it from a rival camp, the Soviet Union would be globally predominant. The West, in other words, can redress the global balance only by keeping Western Europe within its own ambit. That it will do so is far from certain.

II

The European Community is not organised as a single entity for the defence of its own semi-continental region, while the United States, chastened by war in Vietnam and neglect of the home front, wants to do less across the Atlantic rather than more. Some American legislators have called for deep unilateral cuts in her European presence; those who preferred smaller co-operative ones, expected an all-European compact between the North Atlantic Alliance and the Warsaw Pact. But signatories of the Warsaw Pact would not attend a conference at which 'balanced' force reductions were to be discussed. When that term had been struck out, it was clear that Russia, with shorter air distances, will cling to the strategic advantage she also possesses over the United States in having, across the length and breadth of Europe, land frontiers rather than sea frontiers to traverse.

Nor would the Soviet Union be handicapped if the West goes on rending itself. Patently while it is in the American interest to preserve the West European sector of the global balance, it is also in the interest of the West Europeans to do more for the preservation of their own independence.

If, all the same, the United States reduces substantially the number of American troops stationed across the Atlantic, her European allies may still hesitate to fill gaps. That would leave them with one of two options, both grim. As NATO's preparedness for conventional warfare recedes, West Europeans might steel themselves for an early use of tactical nuclear weapons – with a full, all-consuming nuclear exchange springing from it at once. Yet they may not gamble on that. And if they do not, Western Europe could still make a third choice. A deal may always be devised with Russia herself.

And here is the first of a few crucial issues in which, for the defence of the West, much is so upside down. If Western Europe does not yield in a neutralist or Third Force vein to Russian supremacy, it will still depend upon American long-range weapons to withstand hostile pressure. As a supplement, the British and French can muster their nuclear weapons. Against all these, Russia does not only have major ones reserved for North American targets, but is supposed to have 700 missiles, intermediate range, trained on European centres beyond the Iron Curtain.

Anglo-American nuclear cooperation can be traced back to the unique British record against Hitler. The French, however, have created a deterrent of their own, lest the overall American deterrent is withheld when, for saving France or Western Europe, American cities are also menaced. The scene of combat may be Western Europe itself, moreover, when *détente* puts a partial curb on the use of long-range nuclear weapons. And if Western Europe has disengaged itself as a neutral Third Force from the United States, Russia may even obtain ascendancy without striking a blow.

When, too, much of Western Europe no longer rides high economically, it will spend less rather than more for preparedness. The United States, on the other hand, is still the most dynamic economy on the face of the earth and comparative statistics over how other countries have overtaken her should be cited with caution. For what these often disclose is a postwar economic recovery which the Marshall Plan stimulated and not any American economic decline. It is the Russians who have allocated a bigger percentage of the gross national product to the arms race. It is the allies of the United States who, remiss in counting their blessings, have done less than they might to reinvigorate the North Atlantic Alliance.

Before the cold war there were two world wars which demonstrated how little the United States can afford a serious rupture with Western Europe. Yet such may be the upshot unless she perceives that, in power politics, fair is not always fair and that the equitable is not invariably practical.

The withdrawal of American troops from Western Europe has constantly been postponed. What may thus be warded off is the expansion of Russian hegemony to the Atlantic – a contingency the North Atlantic Alliance was formed to anticipate. The position of Finland, abject or semi-abject, is a frequently cited analogy for the posture in which all of Western Europe could find itself – one which allowed more autonomy than Soviet client States of Eastern Europe retain but which, at turning-points, will still have put Western Europe at Russia's beck and call. So drastic a shift in the global balance would demolish the West's power structure. It might also drive an American underwriter of other free societies back into Fortress America – an alternative twice rejected by the United States on the field of battle but which, with all European toe-holds denied her, she may have to accept.

Topsy-turvy would be a statecraft that, by refusing to pay for adequate American troop levels across the Atlantic, invites such a disaster. The United States has been trapped into doing more than her associates by her wealth and strength. The onus of leadership rests on her because, without her, the West could not be led. Is she (as in the lament penned by Mathew Arnold about 19th century Britain):

> The weary Titan . . .
> Bearing on shoulders immense,
> Atlantean, the load,
> Well-nigh not to be borne
> Of the too vast orb of her fate?

She is not. Too great, in spite of domestic turmoil and a neo-isolationist upsurge, is her sheer productive vitality.

European allies (most of whom subjected the United States to a sort of implicit blackmail) have grumbled that, over their heads, Washington and Moscow were negotiating nuclear agreements which might decide the future of all. Things could have been retarded, however, by France and China – nuclear aspirants who did not sign the test ban and non-proliferation treaties. If allies of the United States were consulted this might also have brought into the picture Russia's East European allies, subordinate to Soviet edicts as they are. Washington, all the same, is now reporting fully to NATO about its arms negotiations with Moscow.

So far it is only the rank of those who may sit at the top table that has been publicly touched upon at any summit of summits. In a Kremlin speech on 22 May 1972, when President Nixon bade farewell to the concept of security through preponderance, he admitted that in a nuclear age Great Powers must fraternise with each other as equals. But not all who get such treatment contribute proportionately to peace or world order.

Some trans-Atlantic signatories of the North Atlantic Alliance belong, for instance, to the European Economic Community – an entity which dreamt of operating as a grandiose new unit in world politics but one that could now do more good than harm as a customs union or free trade area. Few of its components are, with their Fabian tactics, willing to make a bigger defence effort the prerequisite to a higher collective status.

Elsewhere, moreover, a country like Japan is not supposed to do so. Nor was it the rapacity of Arab oil States that first embarrassed postwar Japan. Sino-Soviet friction occurs on the mainland of East Asia, and is thus virtually next door. Only China, in addition to the two superpowers, can, through the spartan living standards she imposes on a populace so huge and so restively pinned down, bring full weight to bear.

Nuclear weapons for India, that self-encumbered amalgam of ancient superstition and enlightened modernity, may do less to give new rank and more to keep hostile neighbours at bay. As for the Sovier Union, its Brezhnev Doctrine makes plain that inferiority rather than equality for others is what it desires. And it is curiously upside down when, as the demise of the cold war is proclaimed, the global power balance which Russia elicited must still be upheld. In no other manner, all the same, may the West preclude either confrontation or subjugation. Rival camps do not repudiate the quest for preponderance with deeds as well as words. Until they do, the concept of peace by power will, for free societies, be as valid as ever if free is what they want to be.

Nor is this all. While two world wars taught free societies that they must stick together, the lesson is one they apply with the utmost difficulty. Only at grievous cost did the West learn to identify itself as such and acquire a power structure which has enabled it to sustain its own liberties with those of others in many corners of the earth. This it must underpin. Disruptive, nevertheless, are the inner strains.

And these are manifest in most of the West's intramural proceedings. They cropped up, for example, over currency problems, together with disputes over exports and imports, industrial and agricultural, before Britain entered the European Economic Community. Nor, with inflation rampant, did they improve after the enlargement of that entity. And what was so deplorable about this was that dissension in the economic sphere must derogate from politico-strategic unity at the same time. The more it is prolonged the more is the West's entire power structure likely to be impaired.

Not that, within modest limits, the idea of a European Community has been a mistake. There is everything to be said for it when, with France and the Bonn Republic at peace, components prosper; when too it, with the North Atlantic Alliance, ensures that West Germany gravitates more to the West than the East. But under the constitution of the Bonn Republic West Germans are pledged to work for the reunification of the two Germanies. And if they ever were reunited – a consummation which *Ostpolitik* does not renounce – a greater Germany would so dominate Western Europe that the European Community is sure to dissolve.

Russia has been less than enthusiastic about the European Community. Yet when so much is upside down that entity owes much to her – even if by inadvertence. The Bonn

Republic is made tolerable as a Community member by whatever it is in Russian policy that bisects the former German Reich.

With the close of World War II the Soviet imperium had gobbled up three Baltic States and stretched into Central Europe. As East Prussia and Eastern Poland were Russified, the Oder-Neisse lands were Polonised. When, nevertheless, the North Atlantic Alliance first began and before the European Community had been established, the Kremlin might have set up a loose, neutralised confederation between her own German client State and the Bonn Republic. This would have compelled the West to evacuate armies and aircraft stationed on West German soil. But during its early years the Bonn Republic could not accept a foreshortened Reich. Ideologically, furthermore, its Chancellor, Konrad Adenauer, was pro-Western in sympathy, and most of its citizens were the same. Nor could they be so without preserving Western Europe, as a vital counter in the global balance, from Soviet clutches.

Such a turnabout, soon after Hitler's downfall, was one of history's constructive ironies. The inverted behaviour of the French, by contrast, negated the spirit in which the English-speaking peoples had liberated them, in which the United States fostered among them as among others economic recovery with Marshall aid, and, through the North Atlantic Alliance, rendered them secure at last. After World War II the Fourth Republic spread out a welcome mat for the armed services of its allies. The Fifth Republic of Charles de Gaulle withdrew it and his successors, though more co-operative, kept it withdrawn. When the French clung to membership in the North Atlantic Alliance but stayed out of NATO, its operational apparatus, NATO's political high command moved with military colleagues to Brussels. Henceforth, the North Atlantic Alliance was to lack the hinterland it needed for the defence of French soil and to do without a French contribution to the forward defence of West Germany. Pride made France hug that which pride should have given.

At the moment, however, Russia is unlikely to put these Western aberrations to the test. She has preoccupations of her own. If, nevertheless, the West German boom is deflated and unrest mounts, the idea of a neutral all-German reunion might be revived. Unconditional reunification is an objective that Herr Willy Brandt had, for the nonce, to abandon. But during hard times would the Bonn Republic endorse former Soviet conditions as a harbinger of better days even if they constrain it to turn its back on the West? The postulate here, of course, is the sort of economic slump that released the Nazi scourge. Not that Communist tyranny has been more tender. But the Russian people have a vivid recollection of the demonic impulses that lurk in the German psyche and the Kremlin may be loath to toy with them. All quiet on the Western front is what it desires. This, if another German Reich appears, it might not get.

The map, as ever, must decree how the Soviet Union is to veer and tack. Uppermost, as cartography remoulds policy, are Eurasian inhibitions. When Russia has to cope with China in East Asia she can scarcely approve the rebirth of a reunified greater Germany on the East European frontiers of her own imperium. Bismarck, William II and Hitler are thus not the only ones who have been haunted by the spectre of a war on two fronts or of some pincer movement in world politics which would have a similar outcome. These must also be a nightmare for Mr Brezhnev and his colleagues. Russia, thus, has more than her boundaries with China to defend. Over the Western flank of Eastern Europe the Soviet Union will, in all probability, also stand firm. Elsewhere, though, it might still batten on discord.

III

One source of this in the West has been the advent of the European Economic Community. About that entity the problem posed by the entry of Britain – Ireland and Denmark having also joined – was whether or not it had become too big for the comfort of those who must consort with it. Community components are not yet knit compactly together. Such attempts as they made to speak with a single voice were, for many years, in a French accent. No doubt it could get more practice by having itself recognised as one unit at the United Nations but, except for renewed efforts to scold Israel, it would have little to do there that is on the higher plane of global politics.

Washington had long urged Britain's adherence to the Community. It imagined that, with lesser components, she would keep the Community on the rails. This, however, Britain could never do when she was so hard up; when, with a rise in the cost of living, she still has lopsided budgetary fees to pay. Nor do most of the British people care whether their Community function is to be a higher or lower one. What they reject, above all, is a Europeanising process that may sap national independence – a prerequisite, besides, for historic ties overseas. Then, too, the more centralised the Community becomes the more some components could be dragged by others along a path that they normally would shun. And whatever has enlarged the Community will also have enlarged the zone which Russia might detach from the United States.

It may be a portent, at any rate, that the Soviet Union no longer inveighs as she once did against the European Economic Community. For trade with that body, according to Moscow, Comecon would be a proper candidate. But this is an economic grouping which belongs pretty much to Russia while the European Community belongs solely to itself. It would be good for Moscow, all the same, if discontent in Soviet client States could thus be allayed. Apart from Russia's own new trade pacts with American and Japanese corporations, there are those, preceding Russo-American *détente,* with West Germany, France and Italy.

Through the Communist parties of Western Europe, moreover, the Kremlin has had the tools for politico-strategic access to European countries beyond the Soviet imperium while these enjoy no similar access to it. This is an asymmetry before which free societies, by deep-seated principle, must bend. It is one also from which they might suffer.

Ambivalence in the Bonn Republic derives from its geography. After World War II, West German claims for the reunification of the two Germanies were backed by fellow signatories of the North Atlantic Alliance and thus prolonged the cold war. But the former Chancellor of the Bonn Republic, Herr Willy Brandt, undertook an *Ostpolitik* through which West Germany acknowledged her own postwar frontiers – temporarily, at any rate. And until that succeeded no Russo-American detente could be sought. Distrust of the

Bonn Republic is aroused in the West, however, by a propinquity to the Soviet imperium that is coupled with a vestigial German drift towards the East, one that the deadly peril of nuclear warfare might renew. Advanced countries everywhere want to cash in on Russia's willingness to trade with them. But what the West Germans do in this respect will be scrutinised with the special attention American and Japanese economic activities receive abroad. Yet none has done more than France herself to impair a power structure which renders her secure.

The fact is that the Soviet Union rejoices wherever, as among the French and Italians, Communists have become the most numerous party. Not all obey Moscow slavishly. Where they catch on, however, neutralism is rife and the bulwarks of the West are shaken proportionately. Within the Soviet imperium itself, however, the West cannot give as good as it gets. General de Gaulle, moreover, played into Moscow's hands and so did President Pompidou, when they converted anti-Americanism into a conditioned reflex – though some of this Valery Giscard d'Estaing has assuaged. As for Italy, with its makeshift coalitions of the Centre, there is the nation's sheer ungovernability. During a severe economic setback in 1974, furthermore, she adopted autarchic regulations over which the European Community nearly fell apart. Yet the French, by jeopardising the Common Agricultural Policy, might soon have wrecked the Community themselves.

When Britain joined that entity, a big disgruntled segment of the British people still recoiled from so momentous a step. A Labour Government, in accordance with pre-election undertakings and with the support of many Conservatives, has renegotiated onerous terms for entry. If discontent keeps up a Conservative Government could now do no less. When moderates rather than extremists might let slip the supremacy of Parliament, British political discourse can seldom have been so upside down.

At rock-bottom there is not much that can be renegotiated. The more Britain's sovereignty is usurped by the Community the less right will she have to govern herself. Nor, by the same measure, can she long cherish familiar ties with other English-speaking countries.

And if she decides to resign from the Community, how should this be done – with mutual consent or with a violation of treaties being charged? Britain remains a buttress of the North Atlantic Alliance. Unless she is allowed to depart from the Community without rancour, there may be an uproar from which the defence of the West would be further impaired.

After Britain's exit a smaller Community might be more hesitant about going it alone. An inner threat to the power structure of the West may subside commensurately.

This, with historic Anglo-American rudiments, has been foremost among the political accomplishments of the twentieth century. Certainly it could be more decisive than a United Nations which oscillates between two poles: that of work done by the Secretariat or specialised agencies and that of organs misused as sounding-boards for every kind of ideological malignancy. The more universal venture would not be viable, as a matter of fact, if the West had no power structure. To preserve the latter will not be easy.

And as in global politics so in the field of commerce, a diminished Community could not do as much to bring about a non-Soviet world of closed or semi-closed trading blocs. There are some American neo-isolationists who yet back international trade; what they might gloss over is the degree to which such trade will be less international if some of its strategic girders are kicked away. Rash, too, may be the neutralists of Western Europe, but they could not do as much damage if, when Britain decamps, their style is cramped.

A topsy-turvy wishfulness is what must be avoided once more. Washington, London, even Peking, have conceived of the European Community as a bastion of power against a westward thrust by the Soviet Union. As such China visualises that entity diverting the Soviet Union from her own troubled frontiers in East Asia. The West, rather than China, as Mr Chou En-lai warned, may be what Russia is really after. The Soviet Union cannot, all the same, tackle both China and the West simultaneously. But all bets are off if Western Europe engenders a Third force or a neutralist predisposition – if, manoeuvering between Russia and its own allies, it evades or disavows a basic commitment to the West.

Washington, however, may overlook this danger when it has preconceptions of its own to nourish. A limited liability in American deployment is what the Nixon Doctrine broached, but Western Europe might suppose that henceforth overall American pledges will not be worth as much as they were. Nor has confidence been enhanced by a further post-Vietnam letdown over the Watergate and other national American scandals. The United States may depend globally on fresh combinations and permutations to lift burdens from her shoulders. West Europeans though may wonder whether that will suffice.

In a world of five Great Powers, said Bismarck, it is better to be one of three than one of two. But such an arithmetical truism sprang from a European balance of power which his own Reich was, with the Nazi Reich, destined to crush. Nowadays, when a global equilibrium has supervened, the distribution of power is more uneven. In preparedness for both conventional and nuclear warfare only the United States and Russia are genuine superpowers; China is becoming a lesser superpower strategically before she does so economically. Japanese vacillations stem from remorse over a bellicose past, the cruel trauma of Hiroshima and Nagasaki, the degree to which, as an offshore island, Japan is overshadowed by the Chinese and Russians. Western Europe, on the other hand, cannot qualify as a superpower without a merger and expansion of the British and French nuclear deterrents. For that, from an administrative standpoint, there would have to be political integration. But more political integration is also needed should an economic union materialise.

If Britain pulls out from the European Community, other members of that entity ought still adhere. In the nuclear field, however, Western Europe cannot do much when, as a pivot, only the French deterrent is left. Against the Warsaw Pact, above all, it is in conventional preparedness that the European branch of the North Atlantic Alliance might do more and thus forestall, as the years elapse, crippling repercussions in the politico-strategic domain.

About other aspects of the arms race, it is only an American superpower that can stand up to the Russian colossus. Enmity between China and the Soviet Union enters into the reckoning. Nor would Russia be likely to acquiesce in a major nuclear effort by the European Community unless she were convinced that whatever slackens ties between the United States and Western Europe will foster Soviet global aims.

Washington, from its own point of view, made two broad reappraisals of related matters during the spring of 1973. On behalf of President Nixon, Dr Henry Kissinger suggested a new Atlantic Charter (April 23) but this only aggravated intra-Alliance polemics. Then when the President delivered his annual report on foreign policy to Congress (May 3) the emphasis was on economic differences with the European Community. The inward-looking character of that entity was admitted at last; so were disparities between its economic regionalism and global duties. In spite of this, however, American support of West European integration was reiterated. And indeed at that late date it could not be revoked. But the enlargement of an integrated Community may be something else again. And if the British withdraw from it they may also get the United States off the hook.

The danger is a neutralist or Third Force response on one side of the Atlantic to an outmoded retrenchment, isolationist or semi-isolationist, on the other. Not that Western Europe, as long as it consists of free societies, can actually afford to wheel about. And if that is so, there should be a maximum in consultation between members of the Western coalition. The West is fortunate, nonetheless, that the European Community is neither as well organised nor as well equipped as the United States to contribute to world order – upside down though the merits of such a deficiency may be.

Ever since the Truman Administration, Washington has been enamoured of intellectually neat, labour-saving devices for the unity of Western Europe and Atlantic solidarity. But with these life and politics seldom tally. Baffling, at any rate, was a dictum by President Nixon in his second (1971) annual report on foreign policy to Congress: 'Two strong powers in the West', he had remarked, 'would add flexibility to Western diplomacy.' They may, alas, do quite the opposite. Forgotten might be the axiom that before the unity of Western Europe must come the unity of the West. If there were two superpowers in the West they could not bicker, as a West European aspirant now does with the United States or the United States now does with it, and share the same prerogatives of leadership. Paralysis would ensue. The power structure of the West might be scuttled.

These were hazards at which Washington had long scoffed. They were, nevertheless, to be taken more seriously by Americans who examine the failure of their West European allies to support the United States when war again erupted in the Middle East. On 25 October 1973 after a second cease-fire was accepted, there came alarming news of a world-wide American precautionary alert. If Russia, as patron of the chief Arab belligerents, contemplated any intervention on the spot she had been warned to desist. Such a countervailing move by the United States included the possible use of nuclear long-range weapons as well as conventional non-nuclear ones. The Russo-American confrontation might now be one of the utmost gravity. Yet orders had been given without the views of Atlantic allies, even those geographically so close to the scene of combat, being ascertained.

Washington may have tarried for two reasons. First of all, in a sudden brief confrontation with the Soviet Union, the United States had to act at once; during the Cuban missile crisis of 1962 there was more time to keep in touch with others. On this occasion, too, most European allies had been shunning their own American guarantor. They would not let the United States utilise their facilities when she mounted her massive airlift with arms for Israel; for diplomatic backing she looked to them in vain. Here, nevertheless, they may have been unaccommodating with consistency. An anti-Israel bias was apparent when, a few years before, components of the European Community started to explore prospects for a common or Community foreign policy. Yet, beyond sentiment or domestic politics, it was as much in the interest of Western Europe as of the United States that Israel, like Turkey and Iran, should survive. By her tenacity, she also wards off a Russian stranglehold on the Middle East and thus helps keep Western Europe free.

The North Atlantic Alliance may not oblige European allies to co-operate with the United States over the defence of an adjacent key region. In October 1973 similar global imperatives were what did. And by a firm American stance the strategic limits of *détente,* in the Middle East at least, had been drawn.

There was one deduction, nevertheless, that Washington still hesitated to make. France, the Bonn Republic and Britain were the three principal components of the European Community. All of them had diverged from the United States. As a single entity the Community could not yet stand on its own feet; but, with political and economic integration, it would be capable of doing so – whereupon much more damage might be wrought. And what had been foreshadowed was how, as a unified, neutral Third Force, Western Europe may behave.

At sea, moreover, there were still power vacuums that a British recessional had left to be filled. When therefore the American armed services girded their loins during October 1973, Washington dispatched a carrier task force to the Indian Ocean where it might keep watch on a bigger Russian squadron in those waters and over shipments of oil from the Persian Gulf.

A tocsin had rung and it should remind free societies where their outer ramparts are vulnerable. Only the United States is committed to the defence of more than her own vicinity; only Britain (though France now also keeps watch over oil routes in the Indian Ocean) has had a similar concept of world order. It is as a mainstay of this that the West's own power structure ought to function.

Matters in the West were again bedevilled, however, when Arab oil States thought they might coerce Israel by using oil as a weapon against others. All at once non-Soviet economies, dependent on oil as a fuel, were face to face everywhere with a threat of untold magnitude to modern enterprise and higher living standards. Over the long run free societies can only withstand this and meet warnings from numerous ecologists by self-discipline in the utilisation of natural resources. What should have gone out was a clarion call for wholehearted teamwork by the West. But when so much is upside down little of that could be attained and enough may never be.

In February 1974, all the same, the main oil users, industrialised members and non-members of the European Community were, with the exception of France, agreed to collaborate. By March 4 the European Community, going into reverse, had announced that it would dicker with Arab States on its own.

Secretary Kissinger thereupon reproached European allies for the anti-American vein in which they sought to create a European identity while President Nixon warned that, by its antics, the Community only encouraged the American Congress to bring American troops home from Western Europe. At cultivating Arab countries, though, the United States was no less adept and began to outplay the European Community at its own game. Soon the new personnel in office among the British and French had concurred with the West Germans that the European Community should keep the United States – and even Israel – adequately informed about its own prospective dialogue with Arab nations.

In June 1974, moreover, all members of the North Atlantic Alliance signed an Ottawa Declaration which, after long harsh travail, did somehow reiterate common interests. At last they had formally recognised that these 'can be affected by events in other areas of the world'. The October war in the Middle East thus left its mark. Most of the West Europeans had been willing to let Israel, a small country ostracised by Communists and neutralists, be wiped out; at that critical juncture they also snubbed an American guarantor of their own security. There had, that is to say, been a tentative neutralist Third Force interlude. And if the Alliance could not avert one of these, despite its original text, an Ottawa Declaration may not avert others.

On paper, nevertheless, its grasp of global realities was robust. The Ottawa Declaration pointed out that, for the Alliance, the nuclear capacity of the United States and the European presence of forces from Canada and the United States was indispensable; that whatever defended Western Europe also defended North America and whatever defended North America also defended Western Europe. Yet all this had long been known. More novel was how the Ottawa session had acknowledged that the power structure of the West must be preserved not only from within but on its outskirts. Amd among such peripheral zones is, of course, the Middle East. Yet there, as elsewhere, Washington may overdo the policy inversions to which it, with others, can be driven.

One example of this has been the recent treatment of Egypt. With hasty cease-fires Secretary Kissinger had saved that country from defeat towards the close of the October war and then President Nixon strove to make peace worth her while. But could this not be done without adding to the small amount of nuclear technology Egypt already possessed? In that which Canada had given India there were no safeguards against military use. And as Delhi acquired this capacity it was peddled to South American countries. How fool-proof, in the case of Egypt, can be American safeguards? If these are circumvented will devastating nuclear secrets further pan-Arab objectives? The question, in sum, is whether the White House and State Department did not outsmart themselves. If Egypt deserved aid there are, after all, many other sorts that could be proferred.

Nor is it inexplicable that Israel should be apprehensive. If her superior aptitudes have been converted into nuclear weapons, these will only be employed when, with so much less than Arab States in manpower and *lebensraum,* she has her back to the wall. But topsy-turvy is it again as a protector makes the protected, insecure from the outset, more insecure than ever.

Upside down also may be the notion that Egypt can now always be relied on to thumb her nose at Russia. Even if Alexandria is shut to Soviet warships, they can still use the port of Latakia in Syria. Anglo-American redredging of the Suez Canal was, moreover, accompanied by Russian mine-clearing below the Gulf of Suez.

(It should be noted that Syria allotted terrorists operating from Lebanon the most advanced Soviet weapons against air reprisals by Israel.)

In the Middle East, as elsewhere, statecraft is dogged by antitheses and the art is to see what should be taken from each. Renewed passage through the Suez Canal is good for world trade. By the same token it also gives back Russia a maritime and naval short cut between Odessa and Vladivostok with all such disturbing Afro-Asian implications as this may connote.

As for Arab oil States, they can subsist on foreign investments after progressive economies acquire other sources of oil or adopt new types of energy. Nor in the search for other sources of oil or new types of energy will they, with their recent accumulations of wealth, let the West leave them behind. But it is not improbable that Arab regimes may purchase the infrastructure of modern industry and yet still lack much politically and socially that brought more advanced nations to the fore.

Only the Soviet Union can exploit to the full Arab success in turning so much of global politics topsy-turvy. If Russia controls the land and sea routes of the Middle East it would be more than those who consume its oil that will lie at her mercy. As a natural resource, oil may be a wasting asset. There is, though, sea-traffic in general – the import of raw materials and the export of manufactured goods, commerce between continents and across oceans – over which the Soviet Union can exert sway and without which the free world will decline. Russia might even squabble with Mediterranean client States like Egypt and Syria. In an emergency they may still look to her.

Events, after all, had again played into Soviet hands when the sequel to a coup for uniting Cyprus with Greece disabled the North Atlantic Alliance in the Eastern Mediterranean. For their aggrieved kinsfolk the invading Turks carved out an autonomous ethnic zone, one that could serve as a bastion if the numerous Cypriot Left-wing should ever act with Russia against Turkey on the adjacent mainland. Yet chronic guerilla warfare, reanimated by such rough justice, might deflect Turks from that Caucasian front which they must defend at all costs.

Cyprus, moreover, is the locale of two British sovereign bases which Britain may yet have to relinquish. Here there have been Anglo-American devices for detecting Soviet missile launches as well as Anglo-American facilities – like those at Diego Garcia in the Indian Ocean – for keeping watch, after the Suez Canal is reopened, over oil routes to and from the Persian Gulf.

As for the North Atlantic Alliance, it never could have imagined a conjuncture so topsy-turvy as a conflict between two of its own signatories. Strategically the Turks were stronger than the Greeks and could thus get away with much. Whereupon, emulating the French, a new civilian government in Athens, heirs to the regime of colonels that Washington had supported, withdrew from the military but not the political branch of the Western Alliance. And yet the bulk of the European Community was less ill-disposed towards the United States than it had been. Most of it, quite ready in 1973 to abandon Israel to her fate, was concerned in 1974 about its own.

Anglo-American solidarity, with Britain as co-guarantor of the *status quo* on Cyprus, had sprung back to life. But as between Russia and the West the danger was that the Greeks, with self-defeating pique, or the Turks, if allies reproved them, might work both sides of the street. Yet for doing this, Western Europe also had a potential of its own.

Years ago Russia might have been tempted to move through Turkish waters against the Dardanelles, that historic outlet from the Black Sea. But the vigil maintained by the American Sixth Fleet would still have deterred her even if, with Gerald Ford assuming the Presidency, *détente* did not also beckon. Restraint was the best policy when the Soviet Union, as *tertius gaudens,* needed only to sit back while beyond its own imperium a lot was undone that, since the Age of Discovery, had broadened horizons.

IV

Meanwhile, on home soil, a renewed far-reaching vigil by the United States is not merely strategic in character. One feature of the *détente* between Washington and Moscow has been the promotion of trade. Most favoured nation treatment of Russian imports was, however, a tariff reform that Congress opposed – until, at any rate, the Kremlin lifted constraints on the emigration of Soviet Jews.

The controversy that raged postponed a new American initiative for freer trade. Eventually, this had to come. Even American trade unionists want relief from higher prices and depreciated savings. Now, too, if Britain, sceptical about membership in the European Community, makes herself available once more, the European Free Trade Association may, with most of its former members, take a new lease of life. As the Europeanisation of Britain loomed a number of her overseas trading partners, Commonwealth and non-Commonwealth, made other arrangements. But not all doors are barred and some that are half-open may, with enterprise, have more and more to yield.

Nor should these facts be overlooked when the economic features of *détente* are studied. There are, after all, no precedents, safe or unsafe, for an expansion of trade between superpowers who still vie with each other politically and ideologically. Upside down may be the soothing notion that a greater amount of trade between rival camps will inevitably further *détente* and not detract from it. Such a theory might be a hangover from the Victorian high noon of Cobden and Bright when the Pax Britannica, as a strategic framework, dovetailed with Britain's own new liberal trade practices. And these are still valid for most countries – even when they are more honoured in the breach than the observance. Doubt arises when there is a gargantuan Communist evangel to be disseminated and where, with a ban on bourgeois individualism, commerce can no longer serve as an unpoliced conduit for ideas.

This is not to argue against East-West trade. Where it is mutually advantageous there is, in moderation, much to be said for it. But in terms of power and ideology its growth may not always be mutually advantageous. The argument is, in other words, that the West errs when it grants Russia a trade sweetener for signing agreements on arms control. If these are a boon for free societies they are a boon for her as well. A brake upon nuclear competition will be a blessing for all. Yet beyond that, Soviet insistence upon cosmic bribes should be suspect.

The objection, it may be stressed, is not to commerce in everyday commodities like grain which, as a matter of fact, Russia fancies she will need only over the short haul. There is no secret that for the long haul the West's high technology is what she covets. Here the overriding motive is to get everything that fortifies and nothing that subverts the Communist system. Co-existence, after all, does not extinguish the ideological phase of the global contest. If the West ignores this, as it ignored the plain intent of *Mein Kampf,* it will, for a dire sequel, have nobody to blame but itself.

Soviet policy, if Clausewitz may be reversed, has long been the continuation of war by other means. But it should not devolve on future victims to expedite their own victimisation. 'We will bury you' was Krushchev's dramatic boast. The West might dig its own grave through a wholesale injection of that Western technology by which the development of Soviet natural resources and Soviet industry is to be speeded up.

Against gratuitous concessions to his country there was, in August 1973, a most courageous protest from Mr Andrei Sakharov, celebrated as father of the Soviet hydrogen bomb. Russia, he felt, should be democratised before others could be secure in undertaking a *détente* with her. What had been feared was interference in Soviet domestic affairs. Economic progress, however, was Moscow's goal when Congress, with Senator Henry Jackson at the helm, obtained more emigration rights for Jews and others.

Topsy-turvy was it also when in February 1974 Russia banished the novelist Alexander Solzhenitsyn. She is execrated if she forbids a host of creative artists, scientists and scholars from seeking a haven in Israel or elsewhere in the free world; she is reviled even more when she expels a writer of eminence who feels he can work at home. The Soviet Union torments its best sons whether they stay or whether they go. As with the Nazis, though now by less summary methods, Russia devalues man whatever he does and that is a point to be recollected by all who engage in transactions with her beyond a minimum that save the two superpowers from war.

Such are the upside down features of global politics in the twentieth century that about one thing not even the Soviet Union is wrong. Against an unmanaged circulation of unsettling ideas from the West, a self-perpetuating Soviet cabal could not perpetuate itself. What it proposes is to exchange the tangibles of *détente* but treat intangibles more selectively. When, nevertheless, scientific collaboration verges on cooperation in the domain of technology, it will be hard to determine where tangibles finish and intangibles begin. The

Soviet Union may even put international trade, though it can be weighed and measured, to uses that sabotage free societies.

Statecraft will be topsy-turvy, at all events, if free societies become over-dependent on Russia for much of their energy and raw materials. The oil boycott of the West by Arab countries, at once morally so primitive and politically so retrograde, sounded an alarm that could have a wider application. The maxim that business is business may do for a world order in which, though democracies themselves fall short, they are still pre-eminent. With *détente* there are not the same ideological safeguards, and the power that might be generated by the Soviet Union is on a more ominous scale. Why should the West take such a leap in the dark? It would be wiser to forego profits so as to prolong the profit system and much else to boot.

Nor does commerce always work its magic. Before 1914, for instance, the German Empire, as inventor and manufacturer, shipper and banker, was hardly liberalised by international trade. Neither were Japanese militarists to whom, before Pearl Harbour, the United States sold scrap metal.

Not inapposite, too, may be an afterthought of how the comity of the West has been marred by trade disputes between the United States and such trading partners as Canada, Japan and the European Economic Community. Behind a façade of *détente,* there is plenty to set apart the United States and Russia. It may embitter them all the more in fields such as arms control if they also vex each other over international trade. Arms control between the two superpowers is, besides, at an early stage as yet. It would be best if other *détente* matters could first take their own course.

A boost to the Soviet economy by the West raises unanswered questions. Russia has neglected her own home front so as to build vast arsenals for the fulfilment of Eurasian and global designs. In the Soviet dictatorship, as with the Nazis before Hitler overreached himself, guns have taken priority over butter. There will be no need for these to do so, however, if the Kremlin might resort to the technological fruits of *détente*. A bountiful, open-hearted paternalism can be the impression thus conveyed to its own peoples and even to some among client States together with Communist parties all the world over – one that caters to domestic and strategic demands simultaneously.

Perhaps this is not the case. Beyond a slowdown in the arms race there may be an extra, recondite bonus when free societies do not only bolster the public relations of the Communist system but help it out and simplify for its rulers their multifarious job. But unless there is, the West had better think again.

Moscow hailed the cessation of the cold war and acted as though it were only suspended. Much will be decided by what happens in China after Mao tse-Tung and Chou En-lai have died. If their successors are more conciliatory towards Russia, Russia, as before, could be less conciliatory towards the West. So as to meet all contingencies the West must keep a relatively free hand. This it cannot have if it has leaned on the Soviet Union, as a source of energy and raw materials, unduly.

Backwardness on the domestic sector of the Soviet war economy is what prompts the Soviet quest for trade and technology. The unprogressive conditions that spur on the Kremlin might, nevertheless, yet protect the West from the economic concomitants of *détente*. There are inner checks that may still hamper the modernisation of the Russian home front. Among these Russia is retarded by incompetence on all domestic levels, by a lack of incentives on most. And if that is so the industrialised countries of the West may find voluminous, semi-private transactions with her not only exasperating but unrewarding.

Less comprehensive ones have been tried. Their potential was gauged by West Germans, the French and the Italians before the United States lifted cold war restrictions on American industry and Japan began to haggle with her two giant neighbours on the mainland of East Asia. Payment for new projects, however, may only be with Western credits or by the antiquated method of barter. Perhaps these can be facilitated through joint ventures between the Russian State and corporate non-Russian enterprise. But elsewhere major industrial countries are again trying to liberalise international trade, to promote free market forces. And unless the West takes care it will be undoing with one hand what it does with the other.

As far as the arms race is concerned, the benefits of a slowdown will be mutual. *Détente* economics, however, might be more lopsided. For Russia these could have a politico-strategic utility by which the West would not gain but lose.

Trade between free societies or between other economies that revolve around the West may bind them together constructively. Between competing systems it can induce an ideological trial of strength that the West is not infallibly geared to win.

In Moscow the regime may writhe over the degree to which some professionals are upset politically by contacts with the outside world. Businessmen and technological experts from industrialised countries might sow seeds of unrest when more of them visit Russia and more of their Soviet counterparts pay return visits. But even if some Russians are disaffected by what they hear and see there is little they can do about it. The Soviet Union is more secluded geographically and culturally than countries of the Iberian Peninsula. Even if one or both of the latter swing from the extreme Right to the extreme Left, other parallels, despite a common approach to external affairs, may not be exactly the same throughout. As a police State, the Soviet Union is more diabolically cunning than was its Tsarist predecessor. And, lest *détente* make ideological inroads, the screws have only to be tightened up. Nor is there much about this that, for Russia, is unusual. Dissidents and revolutionaries, as distinguished from discontented national minorities, have always been relatively scant. Two defeats culminated, it is true, in the overthrow of the Tsarist regime. When none or few may outlive a nuclear war, a repetition of 1905 and 1917 can hardly be awaited with hope.

The mantle of authority that Brezhnev and others inherited may not be wrested from them but passed down. Rigour, from humblest to highest is, though, still its adhesive.

What might occur is some modification of the Soviet system as it allows itself, like Peter the Great, another severely controlled opening to the West. Yet when ambitious Party members or unaffiliated young Russians can procure new careers and additional privileges, they may not want to bite the hand that feeds them. Instead of rebelling against the Communist regime they might acquire more of a stake in it. And if they do there will be a broader rather than a narrower base on which it can rest.

For making the most of *détente*, moreover, Russia, with China, enjoys exceptional facilities abroad. Sovietism with a human face is sure to be glorified by the indigenous Communist parties of Western Europe while the old penchant for fellow-travelling may be rekindled among many of those in the West and the Third World who greet salutary experiments in arms control.

Nor can the West stand up to such propaganda before it straightens itself out intellectually. Adverse, at any rate, could be the assumption of free societies that, under *détente*, the ideological phase of the global contest might be treated separately, as a thing apart. This is a view that Russia only fosters when, coexistence permitting, it may pay off. And it may pay off when, over the thrust between power and ideology, free societies lower their guard.

They might even do so, furthermore, when rival camps are at cross-purposes over the terms on which, under *détente*, Russia wants peace kept. An increase in trade with an exchange of technology will not, among others, imply for her all they imply for the West.

'Do not entertain so weak an imagination', Edmund Burke admonished Parliament before the American Revolution began,

> as that your registers and your bonds, your affidavits and your sufferances, your cockets and your clearances are what form the great securities of your commerce. Do not dream that your letters of office, and your instructions, and your suspending clauses are the things that hold together the great contexture of this mysterious whole.

As in Burke's day, so again – the securities of commerce must be put in a broader setting. Trade with Russia calls for prudence, however, not because she is alien to the great contexture of this mysterious whole. Others likewise differ from free societies. And yet at their worst any threat from them can be localised. Against them no global balance has been summoned up. What the West must seek is not conformity but, with or without *détente,* that self-preservation which is the first law of life.

V

Topsy-turvy, then, might be Western statecraft when it quarrels over contributions to the common defence, lets the power structure of the West be recast, or when it employs trade and technology as a bait for Russian goodwill. In most other respects, however, the conduct of policy is by traditional criteria and there its anomalies are no secret. Over some features of global politics, for instance, the West might accept the *status quo* where it augments the Russian sense of security, but not where the Soviet Union quickens its own world-wide aims. Russia, on the other hand, is against change where, as in Eastern Europe and the Baltic, she filched nearby lands for her distended *cordon sanitaire,* one that is an ideological as well as a strategic line of defence. She is for change, nevertheless, where a network of treaties and her bid for naval ascendancy gives her better access to that Indo-Pacific theatre through which she may yet encircle China and, with her eye on the oil of the Persian Gulf, outflank the West. The Kennedy–Krushchev confrontation over Cuba illustrated that there could be no big Soviet foothold near the American heartland. Cienfuegos, a Cuban port, is, however, used by Russian submarines. Beyond the Soviet imperium, to be sure, mere presence does not denote mastery. What, though, Russia probably seeks are fulcra for leverage in regions where the politico-strategic outlook is unsettled. For there (as a British Prime Minister, Lord Salisbury, once phrased it) she might again be pegging out her claims for the future.

Meanwhile, since the West still lives with the consequences of misjudgement before World War II, a reassessment of some current trends may evoke a sense of *dêjà vu,* of having been here before. Should any of these take root, no enforceable initiative in global politics would come from the West. If one does, however, superpowers will have an overriding interest in arms control and in extending this to lesser nuclear aspirants. More debatable are other large-scale transactions with those devoted, under the label of peaceful coexistence, to the abasement of the West. Not until Russia or China revises hostile aims can free societies be wholly in tune with them.

What the West requires are ground rules for some middle ground if it is to maintain its own power structure unscathed and avoid a far-reaching, all-out *rapprochement* with the East that is, as yet, ideologically ill-founded. In Western statecraft, the foreseen may appear upside down; the unforeseen is what might save it from itself. Free societies have their way of life to uphold and it is by this perennial yardstick that, as they conserve power, economic as well as political and strategic, they can best discharge their arduous but inescapable task.

Index